BENCHMARKING

FOR

COMPETITIVE

ADVANTAGE

DISCARDED

Second Edition

TONY BENDELL,
LOUISE BOULTER
and
PAUL GOODSTADT

FT
PITMAN
PUBLISHING

London · Hong Kong · Johannesburg
Melbourne · Singapore · Washington DC

PITMAN PUBLISHING
128 Long Acre, London WC2E 9AN
Tel: +44 (0)171 447 2000
Fax: +44 (0)171 240 5771

A Division of Pearson Professional Limited

First published in Great Britain in 1993
Second edition published in Great Britain in 1998

© Pearson Professional Limited 1998

The right of Tony Bendell, Louise Boulter and Paul Goodstadt to be identified
as authors of this work has been asserted by them in accordance
with the Copyright, Designs and Patents Act 1988.

ISBN 0 273 62634 5

British Library Cataloguing in Publication Data
A CIP catalogue record for this book can be obtained from
the British Library.

1 3 5 7 9 10 8 6 4 2

Typeset by Northern Phototypesetting Co Ltd, Bolton
Printed and bound in Great Britain by
Biddles Ltd, Guildford and King's Lynn

*The Publishers' policy is to use paper manufactured
from sustainable forests.*

CONTENTS

ACKNOWLEDGEMENTS

The authors would like to express their gratitude to all of the people and organizations who have contributed to this book.

We would like to acknowledge, in particular, the high level of co-operation, helpfulness, time and effort shown by the following individuals and organizations:

- Chas McCann, Quality Services at Rank Xerox, Marlow for checking the contents of Chapter 3 in relation to the Xerox experience

- John Brockman, TQM Network Co-ordinator Ministry of Defence in respect of the information provided for Chapter 5

- The Benchmarking Exchange (TBE) for permitting us to use extracts from their Posting Board database

- GPT for giving their permission for the inclusion of the case study material in Chapter 6

- Stuart Haggard, US Department of Veterans Affairs, Captain Donnie Williams, US Air Force & Jay Cavanagh US Department of Energy; authors of Inter-Agency Benchmarking and Best Practices incorporated in Chapter 8

- Richard Parker, Director of Awards at the British Quality Foundation (BQF) for checking Chapter 10

- The DTI for permitting us to publish the Troubleshooting Grid featured in Chapter 12

- The American Productivity & Quality Center and its service, the International Benchmarking Clearinghouse for permitting us to publish the US Benchmarking Code of Conduct and for providing the original material (published in *Benchmarking in Practice,* June/July, 1996) upon which the Bell Canada and GE Medical Systems case studies in Chapter 13 are based

- The following organizations and people who contributed to Chapter 13: Rosalie Bullock and Gurdip Singh of the Law Society, authors of the third case study; and Tony Curley and Neil Keyworth of TNT UK Ltd, authors of the fourth case study. Our thanks go to Virgin Atlantic and the Emirates for permitting us to use the material in the final case study.

Finally the authors would like to thank our publishers at Pitman Publishing for all their patience and understanding.

FOREWORD

One of the reasons why I still undertake teaching and consulting is that I enjoy it, and one of the reasons I enjoy it is that by so doing I keep learning.

Since the first edition of *Benchmarking for Competitive Advantage* was published back in 1993, the 'learning by doing' has continued at an alarming rate. So too has the research. A lot has happened with benchmarking and in the broader arena of business excellence and quality management in the intervening four years. At the personal level, I and my team have been involved in a diversity of applications concerning almost every sector.

This new edition of *Benchmarking for Competitive Advantage* incorporates many new messages from that learning by doing. Key messages include the increasing need to be aware of the legal pitfalls of benchmarking and how to avoid them, the usefulness and cost-effective nature of normal, commercially-available host database systems in benchmarking rather than exclusively relying upon specialist benchmarking centres, and the need to plan and fully integrate benchmarking into management practice to make it successful.

I hope that you find this book interesting, but even more I hope that you apply its information and also learn by doing!

Professor Tony Bendell
Nottingham, England

INTRODUCTION

Benchmarking comes of age

Benchmarking is still a new subject. Despite articles, courses and professional applications, there are still fewer books on it than most other management subjects. 'What is it?' and 'How can we do it?' are still questions that we meet frequently.

Back in the early 1990s when we decided to write a book about benchmarking, few people in the UK and Europe had heard the word; fewer still had any inkling of its meaning. The first edition of *Benchmarking for Competitive Advantage*, published in 1993, was an overnight success. In the week that it was published Professor Tony Bendell spoke on the BBC Radio 4 *In Business* programme on benchmarking. The result was that the *Financial Times* switchboard was immediately blocked by people trying to get hold of the book! In 1994 the Swedish, Spanish and Italian versions of the book were published due to public demand, followed by the Indonesian version in 1995. Meanwhile, in 1994 Tony Bendell contributed to the *Financial Times* video-based Business Toolkit called *Benchmarking to Win*.

> The need now is for both an insight into the role of benchmarking within standard management practice, and a practical understanding of how to do it.

Other developments also took place as the 'benchmarking boom' developed. New books were published and soon politicians were using the term routinely in numerous and often conflicting ways, even within the same speech!

Looking back on those heady days of innocence, it is interesting to note just how much the issue was all about 'concept-sell'. The world was not ready for detail of method, first people had to understand and be convinced of the need. Unfortunately, even today much of the literature on benchmarking has remained at the level of selling the concept. That, however, is no longer good enough; the need has changed. Increasingly, we find people do understand the issue – the *need* for external benchmarking. The need now is for both an insight into the role of benchmarking within standard management practice, and a practical understanding of how to do it.

In summer 1997, Professor Bendell's team addressed the second of these needs by publishing *The Benchmarking Workout* (Pitman Publishing, ISBN 0273 626353). That book brought together the authors' training, consultancy and implementation experience to provide a practical 'hands-on', how-to-do-it guide in order to answer the usual questions we meet in training and consulting.

Benchmarking and management practice

In preparing this second edition, we have attempted to address the other, both more esoteric and yet more important need, which is to deliver an insight into how benchmarking fits within current and developing management practice. This is a real challenge. Western management still has a lot to learn. For the most part, we have not heeded the messages of Edwards Deming: many of us are still too tied up doing, fire-fighting and surviving to tackle the real, strategic, systematic and long-term issues facing our businesses – or indeed, increasingly, public sector organizations.

The old ways based on 'marginal management' have worked until today, so why should we change? Marginal management is about leaving most things as they are, taking them for granted, and just dealing with change 'at the edges' in response to market pressures and change. Putting 10 per cent on sales (compared with last year), taking 15 per cent off costs (compared with last year), improving productivity by 20 per cent (compared with last year) are typical examples of this approach. These issues may be imperatives, but they do not address the fundamental issue of the need for strategic analysis, of where the business is, of where it is going and how to get there. Nor does this approach address what the competition is doing, how technology and the market are changing longer term, and what the implications for the business are.

> **We have not heeded the messages of Edwards Deming: many of us are still too tied up doing, fire-fighting and surviving to tackle the real issues.**

Looking outside the organization, benchmarking needs really to be done in the context of business strategy. It can be done in isolation locally, and be locally successful, but there may be problems of implementation. These are linked to the company culture in which business strategy is not the key driver. The implication of this is that in implementing benchmarking we need to consider the wider issues of quality management and process re-engineering – it should not be thought of in isolation as yet another 'tool'. Instead, benchmarking should be seen as part of management practice within organizations pursuing excellence. And that is exactly how it is treated, within the US's Malcolm Baldrige National Quality Award and the European Business Excellence Award models.

> **In implementing benchmarking we need to consider the wider issues of quality management and process re-engineering – it should not be thought of in isolation as yet another 'tool'.**

The relationship to the recent boom in business process re-engineering or BPR, is more complex. Frequently, BPR has been seen as an external-consultant-run, one-off, blue-sky, green-field re-examination of the business's existing processes. Big-bang, externally done; instead of continuous, done-by-yourself and focusing on process detail, as in benchmarking. As such, BPR may represent a necessary evil – for when you have not been continuously benchmarking and improving and have consequently got behind – but not a desired long-term alternative. Benchmarking, in contrast, involves the people in your business in looking at your business, and outside, and comparing all the time.

Today's benchmarking 'boom'

Benchmarking has become a vogue phrase of the 1990s. Is it just another management fad? The latest fashion? Or does it represent both an evaluation and a revolution in business thinking?

The difficulty of answering these questions is not made easier by the confusion and mysticism surrounding benchmarking. What is this magic new approach? How does it differ from what we have always

5

been doing? How did it help Xerox break through? What exactly do we need to do? How do we start and who can help us? Benchmarking means different things to different people. Naturally, some interpretations are more plausible than others.

In the 1990s it is almost impossible to read a management magazine or attend a management conference without some reference to benchmarking. Magazine articles, conferences and training programmes are exploding in the USA and to some extent a similar benchmarking tidal wave is underway in Europe.

A survey conducted in late 1991 among small, medium and very large US firms revealed that, compared with one year previously, more than three in four of the sample believed that the amount of benchmarking in their firms had increased. During the next five years, 96 per cent of these organizations expected still more benchmarking. It is interesting that the same survey revealed that 95 per cent felt that most companies did not know how to benchmark. Only 28 per cent thought it was a fad.

> **Survey results indicate that leading companies from most industries are benchmarking and that its use is not limited to any one type of industry**

Further results indicate that leading companies from most industries are benchmarking and that its use is not limited to any one type of industry. Most firms also consider themselves to be beginner or novice users of the benchmarking process. Perhaps most interestingly, nearly half of the companies have been conducting benchmarking studies for less than two years, whilst only 20 per cent have been benchmarking for more than five years.

The benchmarking boom has led to an ever-increasing level of requests from companies for co-operation and benchmarking partnerships with others. Interestingly, the US survey revealed that, despite this, 82 per cent of the companies sampled still do not have a formal process for responding to such requests.

In the UK, things are not much different. A survey of the top 1,000 companies by the Confederation of British Industry (CBI) and Coopers & Lybrand revealed that more than two-thirds of the 100 respondents from the manufacturing, service and other sectors claimed to be bench-marking, with 82 per cent of these regarding it as successful. 68 per cent intended to increase investment in bench-marking in the next five years.

Why is this boom happening? Is it structural or will it go away? Various commentators have pointed out that benchmarking is a natural evolution of the concepts of competitor and market analysis, quality improvement programmes, performance measurement and, perhaps most of all, Japanese practices. Its origins may, in one sense, be traced to the early primitive taking apart of products of competitors to see how they were made and how they could be made, whether the same or better.

> **Various commentators have pointed out that benchmarking is a natural evolution of the concepts of competitor and market analysis, quality improvement programmes, performance measurement and, perhaps most of all, Japanese practices.**

This early physical approach progressed one step further when, beginning in the late 1950s, the Japanese visited many thousands of companies around the world, mainly in the USA and Western Europe, specifically to absorb ideas that they could adopt, adapt and improve upon throughout manufacturing processes. The Japanese supplemented their visits to Western organizations with the importation of both Western technology and business practices. This was achieved by the contractual importation of Western knowledge, and between 1952 and 1984, no fewer than 42,000 contracts were entered into by the Japanese. These contracts represented the best technology and 'know-how' that the West possessed and the Japanese put this information to their own advantage, once again using the process of adoption and adaption. They investigated Western products and processes to understand their good and bad features, and then built superior ones at a lower cost. They also transferred good practices and technology used in one business area to a completely different area, driven by commitment to company-wide continuous improvement.

This pattern of extensively purchasing critical technology lasted until the late 1960s, by which time the Japanese were catching up with Western organizations. The success of the Japanese in using

> **The success of the Japanese in using Western technology as a benchmark for their own performance is evident by their international reputation in the commercial arena.**

Western technology as a benchmark for their own performance is evident by their international reputation in the commercial arena. It is difficult to envisage how Japan, a country devastated by the second world war, could have reached this stage without both the contractual importation of knowledge or by visits to the West in search of best practices. A tremendous amount of foresight has been shown by the Japanese in using these two sources of knowledge to their own advantage. Clearly, lessons are to be learnt in the West by building upon these practices used by the Japanese to improve their own performance and share of the commercial market.

When the Xerox Corporation in the USA adopted a similar vigorous approach in 1979, motivated by a rapidly diminishing market share, the birth of benchmarking as we know it today had taken place.

> **The improvement opportunities that were identified and put into place resulted in a swift turnround for Xerox's fortunes and led to best practice benchmarking becoming a central part of business strategy.**

Xerox felt it had no choice. Competitors were able to sell products more cheaply than Xerox could make them. To understand why this was, the product features and performance capabilities of competitive machines were rigorously evaluated and Xerox was also able to investigate the practices of Fuji Xerox in Japan. The improvement opportunities that were identified and put into place resulted in a swift turnround for Xerox's fortunes and led to best practice benchmarking becoming a central part of business strategy. Today, Xerox and Rank Xerox Limited in Europe are generally recognized as leaders in benchmarking in the Western hemisphere.

The lead given by Xerox established the technique in America and it has become a qualifying condition for companies aiming for the prestigious Malcolm Baldrige Award for Quality. More recently, it has become a criterion in the European and UK Business Excellence Awards.

C. Jackson Grayson Junior, chairman of the International Benchmarking Clearinghouse in the USA summarizes the three principal drivers for the benchmarking boom as follows:

1. **Global Competition** As the world becomes smaller, front-edge companies are realizing that they must match or exceed best practices from competitors anywhere in the world in order to survive.

2. **Quality Awards** Increasing interest in the Malcolm Baldrige Award in the US and the new European Quality Award is fuelling the movement towards benchmarking. As an indication, the US Malcolm Baldrige Quality Award requires applicants to demonstrate competitive analysis and benchmarking in 510 of the 1,000 points.

> As the world becomes smaller, front-edge companies are realizing that they must match or exceed best practices from competitors anywhere in the world in order to survive.

3. **Breakthrough Improvements** There is increasing management awareness of just how far companies may be behind global competitors. After many years of having it good, they are only just now getting sensitized to the size of the gap. There is a growing realization says Grayson, that small continuous improvements are not going to be sufficient. Often there are temporal differences between the best and the average in terms of quality time and product development, as well as cost gaps of perhaps 30 to 50 per cent. Most firms therefore, he argues, must obtain large improvements – breakthroughs just to catch up. They are learning from others, he says, that quantum changes are more likely to come from benchmarking than from anything else.

Without a doubt, a major reason for the current interest in benchmarking is a natural evolution from total quality management. TQM programmes have helped us to focus on what we are doing badly and how to do it better. We set ourselves targets for improvement, continuous incremental improvement. However, unless we raise our eyes from the job in hand to look at what others are achieving and how they are achieving it, we may never realize that it is the business processes them-

> **The only way that we can drive our organizations to excellence is to ensure that we keep our eyes on our competitiors and world best practice in all aspects of the business.**

selves, and not just their marginal inefficiencies, which are holding us back. The only way that we can drive our organizations to excellence is to ensure that we keep our eyes on our competitors and world best practice in all aspects of the business. We must benchmark performance and our internal processes by external comparisons against those better than us in order to drive us to improve and show us how to improve.

This book and the meaning of benchmarking

This book, then, is about benchmarking; but what do we mean by that? Today, quite clearly, the term is ambiguous, woolly, a mystery. It appears to require great subtlety of understanding and clearly means different things to different people. Company practices vary dramatically in terms of their implementation or tentative enquiries in relation to benchmarking. Some companies look for consortia of partners to, in some sense, get together and exchange information. Others look for rather broad, perhaps superficial visits to world-leading or comparable companies to get a soft 'feel' for their way of doing things. Others employ consultants, who interpret benchmarking as the collection and comparison of global, primarily financial, measures of company performance. This is often with similar companies in the same industry world-wide, or perhaps, those in comparable circumstances.

Not surprisingly, this lack of clarity has provided a field day for the consultants who 'solve it all'. However, a consultant's report which shows poor financial performance, customer satisfaction or other high level attributes, in comparison with the performance of competitors, does not in itself assist the organization to improve fundamentally. At this global, somewhat nebulous level, much of the problems of organization are well known to the people in and managing them. These measures are fundamentally of output performance, they show how much or how little is being achieved by the organization in comparison with competitors and with world best practice. They do *not* show weaknesses in the internal business processes or strengths. They do *not* show how competitors and world leaders are achieving what they are. They do *not* show what, if anything, is transferable to the organization's particular circumstance

> **Output performance measures do *not* provide an understanding of 'why' – that can only be achieved by personal discovery.**

and how to make that transfer. They do *not* in themselves, provide the degree of certainty that management needs in order to make the step change necessary in their behaviour or style. Output performance measures do *not* provide an understanding of 'why' – that can only be achieved by personal discovery.

Benchmarking on global measures by external consultants does not, and cannot, in itself provide the fundamental insight and change of practice that is necessary to transform the organization from a potential world loser to a world winner. Nor can naïve, unstructured, unplanned, uninformed and often isolated attempts at benchmarking by individuals within an organization, which is in itself not committed to and has not planned what it wants to do with benchmarking. The attractive 'jolly' of visiting another company, particularly somewhere exotic, may be a perk of the job, but such visits are more likely to lead to a petering out of the interest, or even bring benchmarking into disrepute, when they fail to deliver anything substantial.

Benchmarking's real role has to be seen in the context of the organization that is continuously implementing improvement. Modern management jargon might call this a TQM organization, but the jargon itself is not important. Such an organization is continuously looking to improve, and planning improvement. In doing this, it will set itself targets and, for most organizations early in the improvement process, it is most likely that these targets will be improvements relative to its current performance. Often a crucial first step is to identify both what are the key measures of current performance and actually how good a company currently is. Once this is done, targets are established for improvement against time and an action plan put in place to achieve this. There is still, however, one thing missing. If improve-

> **If improvement targets are set without knowledge of what others are doing and achieving, the targets may not be taxing enough to help us stay in business.**

ment targets are set without knowledge of what others are doing and of what others are achieving, the targets may not be taxing enough to help a company or other organization stay in business.

This book's view of benchmarking, then, is not just about the comparison of measures, as it has often been mistaken to be. It is, instead, a natural development of the desire to improve and the process of improvement. As well as looking internally, look for ideas to borrow from those who are doing better, even perhaps in one very specific aspect. In this sense, it is very much an integral part of the improvement process. Nor does benchmarking stop when comparisons have been made and you have been found to be doing well or been found wanting. This is the first step; 'how' and 'why' need to be established, and methods of achievement

> **As well as looking internally, look for ideas to borrow from those who are doing better, even perhaps in one very specific aspect. In this sense, it is very much an integral part of the improvement process.**

evaluated for potential transfer, improvement upon and implementation. Implementation itself is part of the process.

This concept of benchmarking, like TQM, has as one of its central ingredients, the concept of the internal business process. The crucial internal processes of the business need to be identified, and measures and measurement points have to be established. Comparisons in processes and process performance have to be made externally, as well as internally, and process improvement or redesign need to be put in place. Instead of global benchmarking measures, loved by some consultants, process benchmarking becomes the key to improvement.

In this book, we consider the nature of the TQM revolution and the intrinsic importance of business processes. We look at where the TQM revolution falls short and at the need for external comparisons. We look at the pre-history of benchmarking from the various quality gurus, through the history of measurement and we come to the Xerox story; the story of benchmarking for survival. We look at what benchmarking is, and study separately the great benefits to be obtained by the planned use of internal and external benchmarking within organizations.

Public sector benchmarking has not received much attention in management literature, despite the great potential for process and service improvement. We investigate this and also consider the application of benchmarking in some of the more difficult areas; such as research and development, design, management and the creative services sector. The book also deals with the relationship to international award criteria such as for the Malcolm Baldrige Award, the Deming Prize and the European Business Excellence Award. Finally, the book gives the reader some simple 'do's' and 'don'ts' to fight your way through the hype, to help you start the process of implementing benchmarking within your own organization. To help you do this, we provide some simple self-examination forms for you to assess your starting point and build an action plan.

> **Public sector benchmarking has not received much attention in management literature, despite the great potential for process and service improvement.**

Benchmarking taxonomies and classification systems

As part of the benchmarking boom there has been a move by various trade organizations, consultants and benchmarking centres towards constructing and marketing so-called classification systems as an aid to collect, store and retrieve information from various organizations, and in some cases, to develop and protect in-house intellectual property. An example of such a classification system is the US International Benchmarking Clearinghouse's Standard Process Classification, the top-level classification of which is shown in Figure 1.1.

An interesting question is why such classification systems, which clearly do not fit all organizations, are necessary, given the existence of more uniformly applicable and accepted classification structures (such as the clauses of ISO 9000 and the criteria of the Malcolm Baldrige and European Business Excellence Award). Partly, of course, the answer lies in meeting the specialized needs of individual groups or industries, but the extent to which it is happening is questionable.

Fig 1.1 Standard Process Classification of the US-based International Benchmarking Clearinghouse

1	Understand markets and customers
2	Develop vision and strategy
3	Design products and services
4	Produce and deliver
5	Develop and manage human resources
6	Manage information
7	Market and sell
8	Invoice and service customers
9	Execute environmental management programme
10	Manage financial and physical resources
11	Manage external relationships
12	Manage improvement and change

Given benchmarking's origins in the USA and ISO 9000's passage to world dominance developing from the UK, it perhaps is not surprising that the potential between these apparently dissimilar concepts has not been stressed in business literature. On reflection, however, such association may have advantages. For many organizations on the world scene, particularly medium-sized and larger organizations which are more likely to have an interest in benchmarking, there is a need, not just an interest in obtaining certification to ISO 9000. This is a primary requirement that must be put in place to protect their market.

The spread of what was formerly known as BS 5750 within the UK, its adoption as a European standard (EN 29000) and as an international standard (ISO 9000) may truly be said to be unprecedented. ISO 9000 is the international standard for quality systems, which provides a basis for assessing an organization, or part thereof, against objective requirements of organizational discipline and control, traceability and the like. The standard requires that management shows, defines and documents its policy and objectives for, and its commitment to, quality.

Management is responsible for ensuring that the policies are understood, implemented and maintained at all levels of the organization. Responsibility and authority throughout the organization also must be defined, as well as the interrelationship of all personnel who manage, perform and verify work affecting quality. In-house verification requirements must be identified, and adequate resources and trained personnel must be assigned for verification activities. A management representative for quality must be assigned who, irrespective of other duties, has defined authority and responsibility for ensuring that requirements of the standard are implemented and maintained.

The organization must establish and maintain a documented quality system. This must include the preparation and implementation of procedures and work instructions, and must be periodically reviewed by management. Another clause requires that the organization establishes and maintains procedures for contract review. Procedures must be established and maintained to control and verify the design of the product or service, to ensure that it meets the specified requirements. Document control is required.

Purchased product has to conform to the specified requirements and the organization must ensure that this takes place. Adequate purchasing data must be included on purchasing documents. Where appropriate, the organization needs to establish and maintain procedures for identifying product from applicable drawings, specifications or other documents during all stages of production, delivery and installation. Other clauses deal, for example, with process control, inspection and testing, inspection measuring and test equipment, the control of non-conforming product, corrective action and handling, storage, packaging and delivery. Yet more concern the keeping of quality records, the conduct of internal quality audits, the identification of training needs and the provision of training. Where appropriate, servicing or the use of statistical techniques are also covered.

ISO 9000 then, provides a basic requirement in terms of a degree of belief in the organizational integrity of the company. In addition, ISO 9000 may itself provide a benchmarking grid for comparison between organizations. Since the standard categorizes essential aspects of the organization, requires documentation of these in a way which is consistent with the standard and auditable and, to some extent, therefore implies direct comparability of information between organizations, the standard or an augmented version could be used for this purpose.

Following the same logic, the criteria and subcriteria of the Malcolm Baldrige and the European Business Excellence Award models make natural benchmarking classification systems. These models are discussed later in this book. An example of this approach is that used in the recent Agency Benchmarking Pilot Exercise by the UK Government (based on the European Excellence model), in contrast to the specific Government Process Classification Scheme used in US Government. We also discuss public sector benchmarking later in the book.

Getting started: but beware of consultants!

Perhaps most fundamental of all, benchmarking should be a team-based activity, integrated with other quality improvement activities within the organization and closely connected to the planning activities going on at the top. To understand the subject, one might explore and dabble in isolation without real top management support and only lip-service. Once, however, comprehension has been obtained, real top management commitment is needed to make any progress. Here is an area where consultants can be of assistance, since people seldom hear the prophet in their own land. Top management must be convinced and a champion or champions must be found, in order for an organization to take this subject seriously. In the process of convincing top management, of strategically building benchmarking into the business plan and the future, as well as in the introduction of skills, the spreading of experiences from the mistakes of others and in the facilitation role, consultants can be a great help. But they should not do it for you. Benchmarking should be done by your organization, for your organization and to improve your organization. The responsibility is yours.

TOTAL QUALITY MANAGEMENT, CRITICAL SUCCESS FACTORS AND BUSINESS PROCESSES

What does quality really mean?

Even a cursory glance at advertisements on television, in the Press or on advertisement hoardings demonstrates that quality became the 'buzz word' of the 1990s. Furthermore, it has become a strategic issue with major companies putting great emphasis on the steps they have taken to improve the quality of their product or service. Leaving aside any marketing hype, the common meaning and importance of the word 'quality' has changed over the past 50 years. Indeed, according to Armand Feigenbaum, one of the major American quality gurus who introduced modern concepts of quality to Japanese industry in the early 1950s, quality in the West has now become the single, most important force leading to organizational success, and company growth in national and international markets.

What, then, is quality? What does it mean, how has it evolved into total quality management (TQM), that all-embracing improvement culture, and why have so many organizations floundered on the route to its achievement?

Quality is one of today's most misunderstood and often abused words. The meaning of quality is very much dependent upon the context in which it is used, and the perception of the people transmitting and receiving that message. Indeed, the word quality may often quite deliberately be used ambiguously. This brings us to an initial dilemma – that of quality meaning different things to different people, from the performance of a specific product or service offered to the consumer, to the way the entire organization is managed. While the word is used regularly to describe products, and we see advertising for 'quality carpets', 'quality double glazing' and so on, it can and often does cause confusion, since individual perceptions of what quality is will vary. In particular, in organizations, there is a clear need to understand what quality is, since exhortations to 'make quality products' will be interpreted in different ways by different people.

The modern use of the word quality and its high profile originated after Japan's defeat at the end of the second world war. The Americans exported the basic concepts of quality control to Japan, and the work of Dr Edwards Deming, Dr Joseph Juran and others laid the foundations for the subsequent revolution in quality in Japan. Meanwhile, in Europe and the USA the post-war boom was at a height and had created a situation in which the consumer, who had long been starved of essential basic commodities, never mind luxuries, would buy most items offered for sale. It was a production-led market.

Inevitably, the post-war boom years when companies could 'make it and ship it out' came to an end. Markets became saturated and product or service differentiation became less marked. Meanwhile, the Japanese were learning all they could about Western industrialized processes including marketing, finance, and, of course, quality. At that time, it has been said, young Japanese managers came over to the West and saw that we wrote books about quality, made films about quality and gave talks about quality. What they failed to grasp, of course, was that we never actually did any of it! Those of more mature years will remember that during the 1950s and early 1960s the Japanese were criticized for copying many Western products. Consumer items from the Far East were, in many cases, indistinguishable from 'the real thing'. In the midst of their indignation at this turn of events, Western organizations failed to notice that the Japanese were now also improving the products they were copying. More importantly, by this means, they learned a process which was repeatable for the improvement of quality. Thus from the beginning, quality improvement and product benchmarking went hand in hand.

In one sense the word 'quality' is used so frequently nowadays that its real meaning has been lost to many. Used in its traditional way, 'quality' has often been used to denote excellence, beauty or high cost. This rather nebulous and imprecise concept, however, is of little use. A more useful definition of quality is meeting the requirements of the customer, and a necessary first step is therefore to define those requirements. Typically, the word 'requirements' has been equated with 'specification', often ignoring criteria of price or delivery, in addition to product characteristics, so that quality has often been defined as conformance to specification.

However, this approach has several weaknesses. For example, it can over-emphasize inspection which aims to ensure that nothing outside the specification is delivered to the consumer. This can lead to a hit and miss type of operation where the only way of protecting the customer from defective products or poor service may be to put a great deal of emphasis on end-point inspection, which is unreliable anyway. An additional difficulty with this approach is that it takes place when the product or service is at its most expensive, that is, when all the work is complete. In addition, it is also the most critical time to ascertain whether the end product is good enough or not, because the next stage is delivery to the customer, and failure of product or service will usually mean failure to deliver. It is essential to accept that quality cannot be inspected in, but must be designed and manufactured into the product or service. Increasing the end-line inspectors ten-fold will not improve the manufactured quality of the 'product'; it will just reduce the chances of the customer receiving defective goods.

Not only are such inspection processes expensive and time-consuming, they can create a climate in which quality of the product for the customer is considered satisfactory because it passes inspection and therefore does not need to be improved. Furthermore, it does not take into account the changing requirements and needs of the customer, and the market place in which the organization has to operate.

Total quality management, customers and measurement

Early approaches to quality and, in particular, quality control and quality assurance, focused on the product. As Western markets for products became saturated following the post-war boom years, suppliers began to realize that the customer was looking for a total service, not just a product, and therefore the need became apparent for departments such as marketing, design and accounting equally to identify and focus on the needs of customers. So it was that the concept of TQM, which embraced the whole organization, came into being.

From the very early days total quality management (TQM) has meant different things to different people. Some have treated it largely as a motivational campaign aiming to improve service to external customers. Others have focused on internal training as a way of motivating and giving people tools to undertake improvement activities. Many have identified that beyond training, teamwork and the use of statistical techniques there is, in TQM, the quest for the self-improving organization. While cultural change, organizational change and the use of simple tools, together with a documented quality system, all have a part to play, TQM requires a refocus and redirection of the business, as depicted in Figure 2.1.

Fig 2.1 Basic principles of TQM

- Fundamental cultural shift from quality assurance, quality control
- Theme of continuous improvement
- Customer-orientated (internal and external)
- 'Right first time' standard
- Everybody in the company involved
- Led by senior management
- Measure quality costs/critical success factors
- Prevention philosophy
- Supported by quality management system

Some of the organizational issues that may be apparent in any organization are shown in Figure 2.2. There are subtle deficiencies that go beyond conventional definitions of product or service quality assurance. Resolving these is what TQM is about. The purpose is to develop a self-improving organization, that is one in which the rest position is improvement; one in which if you never did anything else to the organization again, it would carry on improving (Figure 2.3).

Total quality management is a strategic approach aimed at producing the best product or service currently available through innovation and continual improvement. It acknowledges the importance of every person within the organization as an expert within their particular role or function, and as the person who has first-hand knowledge of the process and therefore ideas on how to improve it.

Fig 2.2 Possible organizational issues

- No clear relationship with customers

- Lack of clarity on top level objectives and their deployment

- No awareness of cost of quality

- Suspect workforce is under-utilized

- No real measurement of staff performance

- Need to understand the real purpose of the group

- No clear picture of total rework

- No description of output quality

- Redundant procedures need updating

- No standard operating model for the department

Fig 2.3 TQM: The quest for the self-improving organization

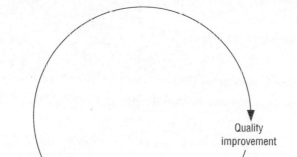

Quality improvement

Entry

Whole organization, every function, every process, every person

In organizations that have treated TQM primarily as a motivational campaign, often there are posters around the walls exhorting employees to, for example, 'Get it right first time'. While this objective is highly commendable, it can often appear as an insult to someone who has worked for a company for many years, and has, as far as he or she is aware, always been getting it right first time. The problem is that often we have not adequately clarified and communicated what the 'it' is that we are trying to get 'right first time'.

Getting started

How to start is simple – as with all project management all we need to do is construct a plan identifying problems and opportunities for improvement, and systematically address these in priority order against a time plan, reprioritizing as the need arises. In starting to execute this plan, different critical issues will be of different importance in various organizations. Those shown in Figure 2.4 correspond to a small manufacturing company, but frequently there is commonality in areas such as the need to clarify vision at top management level, communication problems and customer focus.

In getting started on the path towards TQM we may think of three stages, as illustrated in Figure 2.5. A crucial stage, often in the past strangely neglected, is to start by finding out exactly where you are now. It is clearly beneficial that at the start of TQM implementation the organization undertakes initial data collection, including anonymous questionnaires and independent interviews with members of the workforce, as well as heads of function, in order to identify gaps in practices and procedures, inadequate management, poor communication and problems encountered by people in doing their jobs.

A good way forward at the start of the implementation stage is for a small quality steering group, preferably chaired by the managing director, to be established to manage the path to TQM. It will decide resources, monitor, facilitate and remove barriers to progress. Basic awareness training is now necessary and the board of directors needs to commit itself long term by issuing a mission statement to tell the employees, customers, suppliers and possible other 'stakeholders' which is the path forward. Experience suggests that a 'cascade' model of training rather than 'wall-to-wall' training is to be preferred for TQM awareness.

Fig 2.4 Critical issues

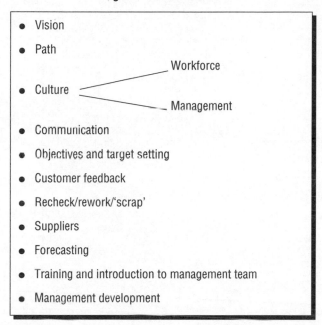

- Vision
- Path
- Culture — Workforce / Management
- Communication
- Objectives and target setting
- Customer feedback
- Recheck/rework/'scrap'
- Suppliers
- Forecasting
- Training and introduction to management team
- Management development

It can be observed that many mission statements issued by organizations bear a striking resemblance to each other and are often taken for granted in the organization. This is not surprising, since after all there are only so many ways of saying more or less the same thing. However, an organization is missing the point if it merely copies another. It is the journey towards constructing the mission statement which is important, that is, the mental exercise for the board of directors of disagreeing, arguing and coming to a common conclusion about what the organization is trying to achieve. Typically, the vision will be of increased profit, increased growth, greater creativity and innovation, and may well allude to the harnessing of the efforts of every person in the organization towards their common aims. But how are these to be achieved? That answer is only by totally satisfying and indeed delighting the customer. While this might seem a self-evident truth, it is not unusual to see mission statements, policy statements or quality policies which totally ignore the customer.

Fig 2.5 Three stages on the path to TQM

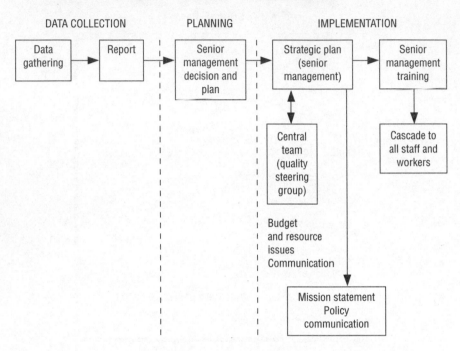

Also, the organization needs to specify what is it that they want project teams, quality circles or individuals to do; what they want them to achieve; it is for this reason that the mission statement or quality policy statement is of vital importance.

Who is the customer?

It is crucially important to the success of any organization embarking upon a total quality management initiative to understand what the end customer wants, and to define the needs and expectations of those customers clearly. However, to many people employed within the organization, meeting the requirements of the customer can seem distant or irrelevant. This is not surprising since perhaps only a very small percentage of all employees ever meet customers, never mind having meaningful face-to-face discussions with them. So how can they hope to understand and interpret their needs? Every person within an organization, whether a secretary, an accounts clerk or an operator, has a role to play in improving quality for the end customer, but they often fail to realize this because they are distanced from that end customer.

It may be helpful, therefore, if everybody within the organization realises that they are themselves both an internal customer and an internal supplier. The internal customer is the next person or department in line to whom they supply work, information, decisions or resources. Similarly, they will have internal suppliers, that is, all those people and departments who supply what is necessary for them to carry out their work. If, at any stage, there is a breakdown in these communications between customer and supplier within the organization, then the quality of the end product or service to the external customer will be less than satisfactory, as illustrated in Figure 2.6.

Fig 2.6 The customer/supplier chain

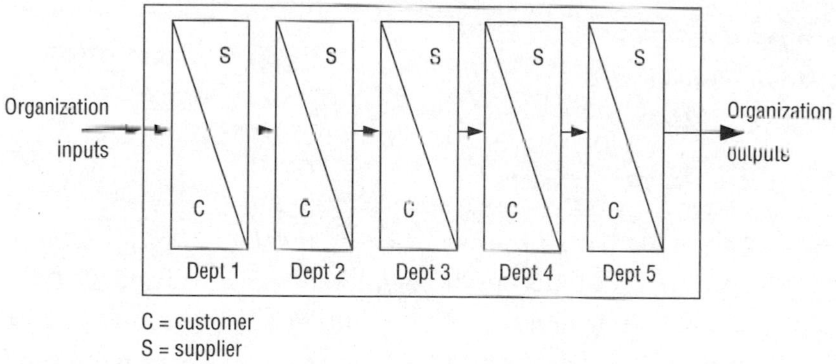

C = customer
S = supplier

A key to improving the operations within the organization is this concept of internal customers and suppliers. Each person is, or should be, 'the' expert at their own job and will understand better than anyone else the barriers which prevent them from doing the job better.

How are you progressing?

Establishing a mission statement for the organization can have a salutary effect, particularly on senior managers and directors. Weeks of discussion and argument, together with several iterations on the statement itself, can lead those involved to falsely conclude that they have now accomplished their task. Typically, the organization will publicize its mission statement, particularly internally to all employees, who will read that the aim is to satisfy customers 'totally' or 'to become the best'. The mission statement, internally at least, will have little value unless it is explained to those who will be involved in the improvement process the role they have to play. The warehouse operator, the forklift driver and the secretary may well all ask (rightly): 'So what do you want me to do?'

Likewise, after two years, how is the organization to understand whether it has progressed or not, and whether there are barriers and obstacles still to be overcome? Unless we can measure how we are performing, at least internally, we will have no monitor of progress towards the mission. At the very minimum, therefore, it is essential that, at all stages of total quality management implementation, clear statements are made to everyone in the organization about:

- What it is aiming for;
- Where it is now.

What should we measure?

Historically, within organizations, measurement has typically concentrated most upon outputs and inputs. Examples of this might be the weekly production figures, monthly profit, final scrap figures or costs. This information, while valuable, can come too late to significantly affect the processes to which they relate. This problem has been compounded in many organizations by the fact that measurement has concentrated almost exclusively on financial data. While the language of money is understood by most people, it does not entirely answer the question of how they should change what they do, in order to achieve better results. Perhaps even more importantly, it does not help them prioritize the key factors which are affecting their output results.

Clearly, some form of measurement is essential in order to monitor progress towards the stated aims and, indeed benchmark performance against others. However, often in the past, measurement is not unified and sometimes appears to be carried out for its own sake. This in turn has led to a plethora of measurements and measurement methods, particularly at the commencement of TQM initiatives, which are unfocused and therefore confusing to those involved. What is required is a unified measurement system which can be used for planning, for monitoring and for driving improvement. Ideally, the measurements used should indicate clearly how the organization is progressing towards its mission, and should avoid the failures of the past in which most measurement was either financial and/or historic and so unfocused as to be confusing. The key to any successful measurement system is simplicity, both in the nature of individual measures and in the means by which it is unified into a coherent, focused whole.

Moreover, it must be recognized at the outset that many employees will have an inherent fear of measurement. This can possibly be traced back to previous unhappy experiences at the mercy of badly-applied external measurement; measurement by those who did not carry out the process itself, but were paid to measure and control the performance of others. If we are to obtain accurate, reliable and meaningful measurement at the point at which it is crucial for control, it is essential that such fears are removed.

From critical success factors to business processes

A unified approach to measurement can be obtained by identifying measureable critical success factors. These represent a small number of key indicators that are such that if they are showing satisfactory progress towards targets, the organization generally will be perceived as being successful on its path of quality improvement. The critical success factors identified should be directly linked to the mission statement so that they indicate progress, or otherwise, towards the mission of the organization. This, again, sets a severe challenge for senior management, since the set of critical success factors needs to be complete in order to convey the total picture. However, they must not be so extensive that they confuse the issues involved. Typically, critical success factors may include measures of profit, cost, on-time delivery performance, sales and so forth. The organization should seek to limit the number of factors to about six or eight, but certainly no more than a dozen.

Having established, then, the link between the mission statement and organizational performance by means of critical success factors, each department and group of individuals can then identify the measurements that they can contribute to improving in order to help the organizational mission. To contribute to improvements in these critical success factors, it will also be beneficial to identify key measurements on particular business processes.

Policy deployment

Often, the approach of CSFs is used in combination with quality policy deployment (QPD). In Japanese examples of the CSF approach, emphasis is often placed upon quality (including service), cost and delivery (including both accuracy and lead time). These can be summarized by the initials QCD. Japanese companies focus on these throughout the organization, including the use of mottos expressing appropriate messages on QCD. Having identified these key measures, policy deployment can be used to translate them into the basis for proactive improvement in pursuit of targets on the measures throughout the organization.

To apply such an approach in the West is a big step, requiring much organizational change throughout the business. Where Western organizations have gone down this route, typically, they have not thought it possible to go immediately and directly to the whole of the unified, harmonious approach. Instead, they have started from the mission statement as part of the normal paraphernalia of the implementation of total quality management. Very frequently, Western companies establish a mission statement as an apparent aim for improvement activities, but then do not provide any direct relationship between the mission statement and the various improvement activities. In consequence, the mission statement can become a hollow vessel; improvement activities can be unfocused and unprioritized; and the usual one-year or two-year crises of confidence or belief can occur in the quality improvement programme.

The alternative approach, which utilizes some of the better aspects of the Japanese QCD approach, is to translate the mission statement into a small set of measurable CSFs, set targets on these annually and over a longer term, and use these to drive quality improvement throughout the organization. This is a much smaller step than jumping directly to QCD and full policy deployment, but still has the advantage of providing a focus for the quality improvement activities within the organization.

Many Western organizations declare that they have CSFs. However, these very often have the disadvantages of not being clear, quantifiable measures, clearly related to the achievement of the mission statement and translatable into focus for all the improvement activities throughout the organization. Sometimes, also, they are called key performance indicators and there are too many of them; more than 12 is too many to remember, to think in terms of, to monitor, and to not get into wrangles about relative weighting.

If one accepts the CSF approach, based on a small set of key performance indicators that reflect the priorities and progress of the business, then it is also necessary to consider their presentation and use. Most effectively, they should be presented and used visually.

Simple run charts, with the desired direction of progress, and clear targets for achieved levels by stated points of time, are highly desired features. This is illustrated in Figure 2.7. An immediate visual impression is presented that helps to see how we are doing. Once established, and the measures validated, any movement in the wrong direction on one of the run charts should be met by immediate management reaction in terms of diagnosis, remedial action, and continued intensive monitoring to resolve the problem. To be used in this way it is important that the CSF graphs are compiled on a current, rather than on an historic, basis. The graphs should be presented, for example, at monthly board meetings to provide a concise overview of the progress of the organization.

Fig 2.7 Present critical success factors clearly

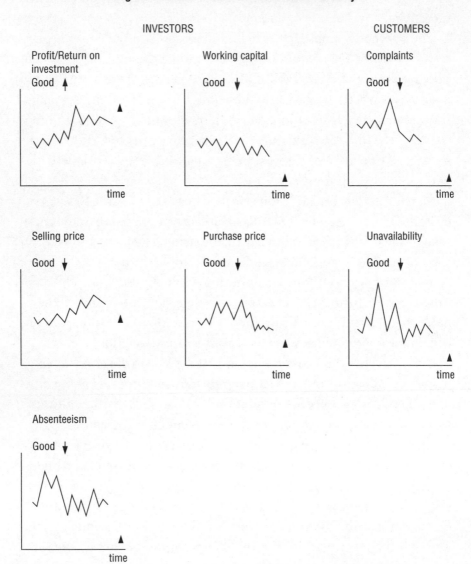

The CSFs should always reflect the critical measures of success or failure as identified by the top management team; these are the criteria on which they are running the business and judging its success. Typically, the ensemble of CSFs may contain customer-orientated measures, as in the case of Japanese companies operating QCD. However, the QCD approach does not, in itself, contain information about the financial performance of the organization that Western management may wish to combine with more customer-focused CSFs. Typically, therefore, CSFs for Western companies also contain profit and possibly cost factors, as well as customer-orientated ones (Figure 2.8). Indeed, the approach may be extended to include factors relevant to other stakeholder groups.

Fig 2.8 Success factors may focus on different groups

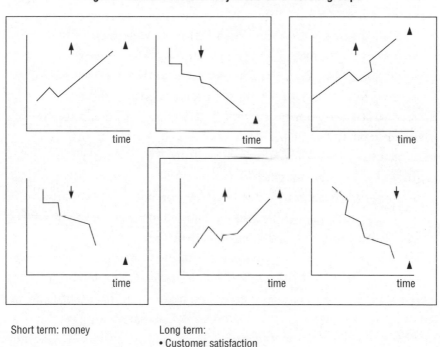

Short term: money

Long term:
• Customer satisfaction
• Other stakeholders

Business processes

Having identified and measured critical success factors, these can be used for target setting, monitoring and strategic benchmarking. To deliver actual improvement there will now be a need to examine and improve the business processes – all the value-adding activities within the organization.

What is a process?

Processes can be defined as mechanisms by which inputs are transformed into outputs. Outputs may well include a service, product, paperwork or materials, which differs from the original inputs. For example, the generation of a purchase order to a supplier may well involve several different stages or process steps. Each of these stages, typically, will belong to different personnel or different departments and no one person within the organization may be responsible for the total process, other than the managing director. Historically, most organizations have been structured on a vertical, departmental or functional model. However, most processes within the organization flow across the organization, that is horizontally, passing from department to department or person to person. It is not surprising, therefore, that the external customer very often does not receive what was requested. Many business processes may be likened to a relay race, with the baton passing from person to person within the organization. As in a relay race in real life, the problems occur at the interfaces or changeover points where the baton is dropped.

Identifying key business processes, the owners and the boundaries of each part of the process are key elements in the implementation of TQM. There are techniques available to assist with this identification, such as 'process deployment flowcharting'. In satisfying this requirement for the clarification and simplification of processes, where they already exist documented quality management systems such as ISO 9000 may be a good start.

To monitor the progress of the organization towards its goals, various types of business process measurement may be used. *Effective-*

ness measures how good the output is from the process. One aspect of this is *accuracy*, i.e., is it correct or not, if so by how much? *Reliability* tells us how frequently it is correct and *timeliness* indicates whether it is late, and by how much. *Volume* is also important and *efficiency* and *cost* tell us how well resources are used.

While the above types of measurement are appropriate at the end of the process, it is far more important to use them at the end of each process stage, internally to the process itself. This will assist the organization in ensuring early that the outcome to the ultimate customer is satisfactory. Process measurement can also provide feedback which gives an individual or a department the opportunity to improve while the work is being performed, so that they can correct the parameters within their control. Feeding back information in this way directly into the process enables two possible savings to be made:

- Employees do not continue to make errors;
- Resources are not added to an already effective system.

It is essential that process measurements are taken as close as possible to the source of any potential errors or ineffeciencies, etc. Some measurements may be only taken for a short time, whilst examining current performance, for example where a particular parameter or performance level is difficult to measure. This will ensure that disruption to process flow is minimized.

To identify a process then, we must look at the provision of product or service to a customer and the steps to provide it; we must ask how it is delivered and follow the workflow through the organization, from first input stage. To describe a process, some sort of flowcharting is particularly useful or we can rely on procedure writing such as is common in quality assurance systems and implementing ISO 9000. To analyze processes, we can look at those flowcharts, at the exception paths and the boundaries, and all other aspects, and so to identify deficiencies. These may include 'holes' in the process when certain peculiar circumstances occur, unnecessary repetitive operations, clear organizational inefficiencies, inherent lack of customer contact, overcomplicated procedures of a bureaucratic nature and lack of ownership. We can also monitor and measure the processes with a view to an improvement in performance and customer satisfaction.

To put such measurement into place, the crucial thing is that we must have a clear consensus as to why it is necessary and how we are going to do it. Top management must be clearly and visibly behind it, and they must take the trouble to explain to the organization what it is, why it is being implemented and how.

Business processes and benchmarking

Before embarking on benchmarking it is essential that you become familiar with your own internal business process. In fact, knowledge of an organization's internal business processes is cited by a US Benchmarking Clearinghouse survey as being one of the most important factors for benchmarking, with 98 per cent of the organizations which took part in the survey seeing this factor as being of great or very great importance to a successful study. A major part of this is understanding what the CSFs in your company are, i.e., those factors upon which the success or failure of the organization can be measured. If you do not know what they are, then it naturally follows that you will not know which processes to benchmark.

Full familiarization with an organization's internal processes is lengthy and dependent, of course, on how large the organization is. One of the pitfalls is not following this process through thoroughly. This can sometimes mean that the benchmarking team arranges an external visit to collect information before it is actually ready to make the best use of the visit. These visits result in frustration, with management receiving data of no relevance, making for a needless, wasteful, and disappointing journey.

Process analysis and flowcharting

How then should the business go about identifying, describing and analyzing processes? The identification stage is time-consuming, repetitive, and sometimes fraught. As with so much else in TQM, the basic technique is to assemble a group with an understanding of the process between them and to extract from the group local information, to enable the process to be adequately described. In carrying out this operation, flowcharting is extremely valuable, since it provides a visual, and yet documented, version of the process being described. Once a draft flowchart section is suggested on how that stage of the process works, it becomes much easier for other members of the team to identify mistakes in conception, in the description of the internal processes. Further, they can identify negative paths or recycling where what should happen has not happened, and so suggest what remedial action needs to be taken.

Such negative paths are one of the major issues associated with the process view of organizations. The unusual document that requires a bit of thought, or inquiry of others, which stays in the corner of a desk for an indefinite period, is a classic example of this type of problem. Unfortunately, such an unusual document may well experience these sorts of problems at various stages in its transition through the organization, leading to enormous delay and confusion for the customer expecting the service. Indeed, when something starts to go wrong within an organization, processes have often not been established to deal with these complexities, and intelligent human intervention is deemed to be necessary. No process documentation may exist under these circumstances.

With a flowchart, problems and bottlenecks can be quickly identified. If there are conflicts or delays between the different departments, anomalies in the procedure will also be identified.

If there is a perceived time problem in getting the product or service delivery through all process stages, it may be worth involving a process engineer to identify the times that a product should be at each stage of the process, then compare them with the actual. It may be that delays are due to the process time constraints; it may also be that the product spends 90 per cent of its process time waiting for the next stage. All of these aspects need to be investigated, analyzed and improved upon.

Traditionally, the output of the process receives attention, because the emphasis in the past has been on inspection or detection, rather than prevention. Unfortunately, this is an expensive way forward. By ensuring that the process is in control, that the inputs are always capable of meeting the requirements of the process, and that the process will only produce correct product or service, detention costs and rectification costs will be reduced.

In this model of things, process control is also important for monitoring, and for forecasting of eventual cost, time scale, and problem handling.

Process deployment flowcharts

An example of process deployment flowcharts is given in Figure 2.9. It also shows the symbols used when constructing flowcharts. Novel aspects of process deployment flowcharting are that the horizontal dimension is used to define the cast of characters, and negative paths and recycling are shown by dashed lines. With these two features in place, process deployment flowcharts become invaluable for describing processes; for helping present procedures (such as in gaining certification to ISO 9000); for clarifying issues about cost of quality; for identifying measurement points in the internal business processes; for seeing those business processes unambiguously, (probably for the first time), and for use in benchmarking.

In Figure 2.9 we can see that a task initiated by department X is described in more detail elsewhere, but is carried out in consultation with Mr A. Once a task has been completed, department X issues a report (depicted by a sheaf of papers), and then calls a meeting with department Y, department Z and in consultation with Mrs B and the customer. The meeting is indicated by the oval shape. Following the meeting, Mrs B initiates action and decides the outcome. If the outcome is a positive one, department X minutes the meeting and Mrs B, together with Mr A, do a standard task, led by Mrs B. However, if the outcome is a negative one, then the ball passes back to department X to do the initial task again, in consultation with Mr A.

Fig 2.9 A process deployment flowchart

The cast of characters

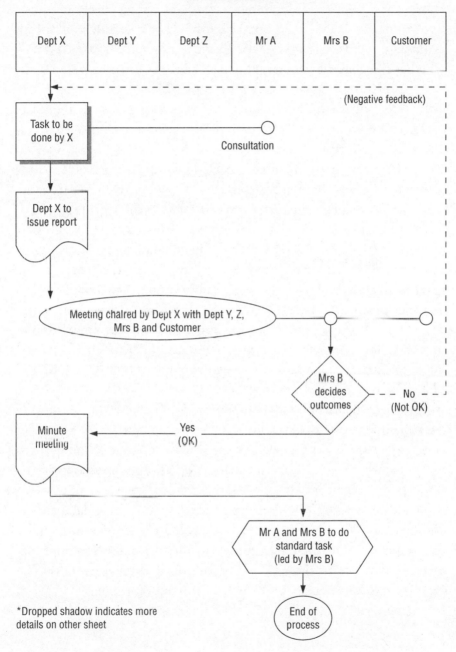

*Dropped shadow indicates more details on other sheet

The need for external comparisons

Having analyzed its business processes, and put in place key measurements, the TQM-based organization will be carefully monitoring progress towards its stated goals. However, the question arises as to whether the goals have been set realistically, yet in an unbiased manner. Equally importantly, the rate of improvement will also be a crucial factor since, if competitors are improving faster, then the organization will be left behind. Typically, as in the case of financial budgets for example, targets may have been set on the basis of an internal view of 'better than last year'. This marginal management is somewhat akin to steering the ship by looking out over the stern!

Today, for many businesses, competition is on the world stage and, in the critical areas selected, the only sensible goals are 'world best practice' or world class. For many other companies, competing in smaller arenas, the targets may not always be as stringent, but the need for realistic goal-setting is just as important. Benchmarking is a method for making sure that targets are relevant to market demands and not arbitrarily established by a finger in the air or an extrapolation from last year's achievements. The technique is equally applicable in manufacturing and service organizations, and in the public and private sectors.

Making comparisons with competitors is not a new idea. Acquiring data about how one's competitors are performing, what their product range comprises, what prices they are able to command, and perhaps their operating methods, has always been part of the marketing function's *modus operandi*. Benchmarking today, however, is much more sophisticated than a furtive, mainly reactive, short-term data-gathering exercise. Instead, it is a highly-respected proactive management tool which is increasingly being used to identify and focus improvement activities with the goal of international competitiveness. The Japanese, perhaps, made it into an art form and Xerox gave it a Western name.

ORIGINS AND THE DEVELOPMENT OF BENCHMARKING

From where did benchmarking come?

Throughout history, people have developed methods and tools for setting, and hence maintaining and improving, standards of performance. One can trace the desire to improve performance and the actual process of improvement as far back as the early civilizations; from the ancient Egyptians who developed accurate methods of measurement by the use of a tool, referred to as the 'royal cubit', to the ancient Greeks who left us with exemplars of architecture, art and design, to the Romans who built upon the achievements of both the Egyptians and Greeks by developing the ability to construct bridges and roads to standardized designs.

To understand the evolutionary development of benchmarking, in this chapter we put it into context of earlier quality themes; from the early development of standards in relation to the control of quality, the development of statistical process control, the emergence of the quality gurus and total quality management, to the early approach by the Japanese to benchmarking. In a very real sense, benchmarking is a natural evolution from principles of quality measurement and TQM; the natural next step in a story that began before the Industrial Revolution.

Early development of standards for the control of quality

During the early part of the Middle Ages, associations were established by master craftsmen. They were established not only to enhance and protect their members' livelihoods, but also for the maintenance of standards in relation to quality. This was taken a stage further by the introduction of the Guild Act of England which appointed 'wardens' to ensure that work was of an acceptable level. Both of these controls were an early means of quality control in relation to the products being produced.

Towards the middle of the eighteenth century there was a shift in emphasis in relation to the type of work which was being carried out, with a move away from the work being produced by craftspeople and a move towards factory-based processes. The majority of the working population was consequently involved in the operation of machinery, the advent of what we now identify as the Industrial Revolution.

During this period one can point to people's desire to improve performance and maintain quality. This is exemplified by the inventor of the cotton gin (a machine used for mechanically extracting cotton fibre from seed pods), Eli Whitney (1765–1825), who applied mass production techniques to the manufacturing of 10,000 muskets for the US army. The creation of jigs, templates and moulds had the effect of ensuring that all manufacturing parts were identical and therefore interchangeable. This resulted in the whole assembly operation being speeded up, with Whitney undertaking an analysis of workloads to determine how many operators a supervisor could manage effectively.

Frederick Winslow Taylor (1856–1917), another American, developed Whitney's production methods a stage further. Taylor developed a system now referred to as 'scientific management' or 'Taylorism'. Stop-watches were given to foremen and jobs were broken into their component elements; times to achieve an optimum performance were recorded which then became work standards.

During this time, not only was the production process speeded up, but the maintenance of quality also became regulated. It is no surprise that, by the end of the nineteenth century, as a consequence of Taylorism, supervisors had more people reporting to them and, so that supervisors could concentrate more on production issues, it became common for the quality to be checked by inspectors who had no direct involvement with, or responsibility for, the production process.

The development of statistical quality control

The requirements for mass production were accelerated by the onset of the first world war. As a consequence, mass production brought with it more inspection in the production process. In response to this, the Technical Inspection Association was formed shortly after the war in the UK and was subsequently incorporated as the Institute of Engineering Inspection in 1922 and later became the Institute of Quality Assurance in 1972. Nevertheless, inspection is not a wholly reliable method of quality control and, not only is it time-consuming, it is also expensive in terms of person power.

A consequence was the development of Statistical Quality Control. In the 1920s in the USA, Western Electric (telecommunication giants) established an Inspection Engineering Department at its Bell laboratories in New York. It was here that Dr Walter A. Shewhart, generally regarded as the originator of statistical quality control, designed the first control charts, and applied statistical methods to the measurement and control of quality.

Shewhart's control charts necessitated the application of quality measurement and quality control at the point of manufacture instead of at the end of the line. Instead of inspection being carried out at the end of the line, critical steps in a process were sampled regularly, measurements taken and recorded chronologically on control charts. Various chart interpretation rules have been developed which allow the process operator to establish whether or not the process is in statistical control or not. Where there is non-conformance of a product the process can be stopped and the cause of the 'out of control' condition may be investigated and remedied before resuming production. Any excessive incidence of non-conforming product is consequently prevented during the process, instead of being appraised at the end of the process. The advantages of this are numerous, since there is a reduction in non-conforming product, as well as a saving in costs.

Shewhart's methodology can also bring about additional improvements in quality. Shewhart stressed that there was a difference between 'common' causes of variation and 'special' or 'assignable' causes of variation. 'Common' causes of variation may be defined as being part of the system and beyond the operator's control, while 'assignable' causes of variation may be caused by specific circumstances. The initial work of setting up the control charts necessitates the removal of as many special causes as possible, so that the process runs in statistical control, demonstrating only common causes of variation. Additional special causes may present themselves for removal, and also management can take steps to remove some of the common causes and thus improve the overall variability of the process.

In 1925, one of Shewhart's colleagues, Harold E. Dodge, developed statistically-based methods of acceptance sampling: methods which allow the user to get an accurate appreciation of the quality of a consignment by inspecting and measuring only a part of it.

The second world war and the emergence of the quality gurus

The second world war was responsible for the establishment of statistical techniques of measuring, evaluating and controlling quality, both in the USA and in the UK. From this, the principles of quality management were established, and is what we now know today as total quality management. TQM is now recognized as being one of the factors which has been such a driving force in the establishment of the Japanese as international exporters.

Since the second world war, various 'quality gurus' have made significant contributions to quality methodology and thinking. These are individuals who have led to the development of what we now call TQM and its caveat, benchmarking.

The gurus discussed in this chapter are Deming, Juran, Feigenbaum (the key American gurus who visited Japan shortly after the second world war); and Ishikawa, Taguchi and Shingo, the Japanese gurus. All of these have made significant contributions in the field of quality improvement.

Dr W. Edwards Deming

Edwards Deming was born in 1900, in Iowa, USA, and was awarded his doctorate in mathematical physics from Yale in 1928. He joined the US Department of Agriculture and in 1936 he came to England to study for a time under R. A. Fisher, who developed the statistical design of experiments.

Deming had met Shewhart in 1927 and worked closely with him thereafter. Whereas Shewhart had concentrated on manufacturing processes, Deming believed that the same concepts could be applied in other areas. In 1939, when Deming moved to the National Bureau of the Census, he applied Shewhart's statistical techniques to routine clerical operations. This resulted in some processes showing a six-fold productivity improvement, massive savings and the census report being published earlier than usual.

Attempts to meet the increased demands in materials for the war effort in America meant that many unskilled personnel were recruited by the manufacturing industries. Quality levels fell as a result and, in 1942, courses to teach various statistical approaches for the measurement and control of quality were quickly organized throughout the US, some 31,000 personnel undergoing training. Both Deming and Shewhart were active in this effort and Deming himself led 23 courses. His training in his own and Shewhart's methods, to designers, inspectors and engineers, resulted in substantial reductions in scrap and rework, together with productivity improvements. (Several people involved with this training programme banded together in 1946 to establish the American Society for Quality Control.)

The gains in the use of statistical techniques for quality control made during the war were short-lived, both in the USA and the UK. In the boom market that developed, everything would sell, regardless of quality. Furthermore, many of the managers running the factories were not fully committed to the approach. To quote Deming from Nancy R. Mann's *The Keys to Excellence: The Story of the Deming Philosophy*, (London, Mercury, 1989);

> The courses were well-received by engineers, but management paid no attention to them. Management did not understand that they had to get behind improvement of quality and carry out their obligations from the top down. Any instabilities can help to point out specific times or locations of local problems. Once these local problems are removed, there is a process that will continue until someone changes it. Changing the process is management's responsibility. And we failed to teach them that.

Shortly after the war, Deming went twice to Japan to assist Japanese statisticians in studies of housing and nutrition, and for preparation of the census of 1951. It was during these visits that he met members of JUSE, the Union of Japanese Scientists and Engineers, which had been founded in 1946 to aid the rebuilding of Japan. A delegation from Bell Telephone Laboratories also visited Japan at about this time to demonstrate how the statistical methods, as developed and taught by Shewhart and Deming, could be used for controlling and improving quality in the Japanese telecommunications industry. Deming was invited to Japan again, this time by JUSE.

The Japanese were aware of British Standard 6000 and also the Z-I American Standards developed during the war, but because the statistical approach was difficult to understand, it was not accepted widely. Ishikawa, in *What is Total Quality Control? The Japanese Way*, (London, Prentice Hall, 1985), wrote;

> In management, Japan also lagged behind, using the so-called Taylor method in certain quarters ... Quality control was totally dependent on inspection, and not every product was sufficiently inspected. In those days Japan was still competing with cost and price but not with quality. It was literally still the age of 'cheap and poor' products.

Deming returned to Japan in June 1950 and taught more than 500 managers and engineers about the importance of understanding and controlling variation, and the use of control charts, in a series of eight-day courses. He also introduced a systematic approach to problem solving and improvement, known variously as the Shewhart cycle (by Deming himself), the Deming cycle and the PDCA cycle. This Plan, Do, Check, Action cycle shown in Figure 3.1, is an improvement methodology involving a feedback loop. The normal tendency, without the discipline imposed by the cycle, is to skimp on the planning and checking phases (target setting and monitoring), and perhaps to concentrate on the doing element. This leads to reacting or fire-fighting, instead of a controlled assessment of the situation and then further action based on fact. It has been suggested that this may be because of the results-orientated society of the West, where doing is seen as being productive (and is easily measurable) and planning may be seen as procrastination.

Fig 3.1 The PDCA (Plan, Do, Check, Action) cycle

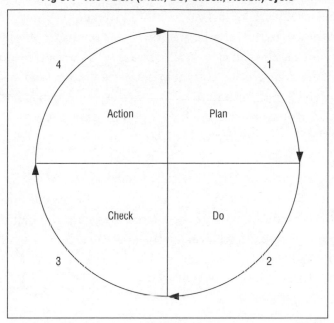

Deming was determined to avoid a repetition of the situation that he had seen develop in America after the war. He made arrangements through JUSE to address senior managers to make them aware of the roles and responsibilities that they must take on board if Japanese industry was to turn itself around by making improvements in its quality performance to compete internationally. He stressed the need for working closely with suppliers to improve the uniformity and reliability of incoming materials, and also the need for maintenance of equipment.

He also emphasized the importance of the customer and, in subsequent visits in 1951 and 1952, when he addressed many more engineers and top managers, he supplemented his usual courses with lessons on customer research and modern methods of sampling. He taught that 'the customer is the most important part of the production line' and his courses committed his students to carrying out door-to-door surveys in order to measure consumer requirements.

In the West, it was not until the 1970s that Deming started to make an impact. In 1980 when NBC, the American broadcasting company, made a documentary entitled *If Japan Can, Why Can't We?* many more became aware of his concepts. However, Deming was constantly reviewing and refining his ideas, and his later work is more management-based than statistically based. His famous 14 points for management were produced to help people to understand and implement 'the total transformation of Western style of management' that he believed to be necessary. The 14 points, and more of Deming's later thinking, are captured in his 1986 book, *Out of the Crisis* (Cambridge University Press, 1986).

Deming was awarded the Shewhart Medal by the American Society for Quality Control in 1956 and, in 1960, he became the first to be awarded the Second Order of the Sacred Treasure, the highest decoration that can be conferred on a non-Japanese. He was awarded the National Medal of Technology in America in 1987. He died on December 20, 1993 at the age of 93.

Dr Joseph M. Juran

Another recipient of the Second Order of the Sacred Treasure, though not until 1980, is Joseph Juran. Juran was born in Romania in 1904 and moved to America at an early age. He trained as an engineer, but his career has been varied; industrial executive, government administrator, university professor, labour arbitrator, corporate director and management consultant. He went to Japan in 1954, also at the invitation of JUSE.

His broad experience in management, coupled with his expertise in quality methods, meant he was able to discuss the wider issues of quality measurement and to appeal to senior Japanese managers. His lectures focused on planning and organizational issues, management's responsibility for quality, and the need to set goals and targets for improvement. He emphasized that quality control should be an integral part of management control. His lectures were followed up at more junior management levels by JUSE and the Japanese Standards Association. Large companies started internal training, courses for foremen were offered on national radio and booklets were made available at newspaper kiosks.

In the first edition of the *Quality Control Handbook* (New York, McGraw Hill, 1988), Juran used the phrase 'There is gold in the mine'. This was a reference to the huge cost saving that can be made by measuring and resolving quality problems. However, it is not at the surface; you have to dig for it. Juran knew that making quality improvements was not easy; there are many barriers and obstacles to be overcome. Juran has used the measurement of costs attributable to quality problems within an organization to capture the attention of senior management in the West.

Quality costs can also be used to prioritize and monitor improvement activity. Juran believes that at least 80 per cent of quality problems result from the systems and procedures laid down by management, so exhortations to the workforce to try harder will only serve to alienate them. Instead, he advocates the use of cross-functional management teams for achieving quality improvement. He teaches a project-by-project approach to solving quality problems and was probably the first to recommend the use of the Pareto principle for prioritizing actions; identifying and tackling the 'vital few' problems and not the 'useful many'.

Juran also stresses the need for planning for quality. He sees quality planning as part of the quality trilogy of quality planning, quality control and quality improvement.

Quality control is the responsibility of the operating personnel, maintaining the *status quo* by following procedures, monitoring outputs and fire-fighting if necessary. Quality improvement has already been discussed, and it concerns the measurement and reduction of what Juran calls chronic quality problems.

Quality planning uses the lessons learned while making improvements to ensure that similar problems are avoided in the future. In *Juran on Planning for Quality* (New York, The Free Press, 1988), the key elements in implementing company-wide strategic quality planning are seen as identifying customers and their needs; establishing optimal quality goals; creating measurements of quality; planning processes capable of meeting quality goals under operating conditions; and producing continuing results in improved market share, premium prices, and a reduction of error rates in the office and factory.

Each stage of the planning process has inputs and outputs. Throughout the process there is a series of suppliers (of the inputs) and customers (for the outputs). Juran sees these supplier-customer relationships extending beyond the planning phase and on through all the steps involved in actually supplying the goods or service to the end user or consumer. The public in general may be regarded as a customer if the product or service (or the provision of it) affects it sufficiently.

Measurement must be introduced throughout this supplier-customer chain to evaluate, control and improve what the customer (internal or external) receives. The type, frequency and method of measurement will depend on the stage of the process and the people who will use it.

Juran, like Deming, has been critical of senior management in the West, but he sees the 1990s as the time when the improvement efforts made by Western organizations over the last decade will finally bear fruit.

Dr Armand V. Feigenbaum

Armand Feigenbaum was the third major American quality expert to visit Japan in the 1950s. Now in his seventies, he was somewhat younger than Deming and Juran. In the 1950s, as head of quality at the General Electric Company, he had extensive contacts with Japanese companies such as Toshiba and Hitachi, and his 1951 book was translated into Japanese.

Feigenbaum argued for the involvement of all functions within the quality process, not just the manufacturing area. The idea was to build quality in at an early stage instead of relying on process control and inspection further down the line. His concept of total quality control extends the administrative function to include the measurement and control of quality at every stage, from customer specification and sales, through design, engineering, assembly and shipment. In *Total Quality Control*, published in 1983, he states that 'Quality is in its essence a way of managing the organization'. More recently, Feigenbaum sees quality as having become the single, most important force leading to organizational success and company growth in national and international markets.

Feigenbaum teaches that effective management of the factors affecting quality means that control procedures must be in place throughout the production or service process including:

- New design control;
- Incoming material control;
- Product control;
- Special process studies.

In *Quality Control: Principles, Practices and Administration*; he defines quality control as:

> An effective system for co-ordinating the quality maintenance and quality improvement efforts of the various groups in an organization so as to enable production at the most economical levels which allow for full customer satisfaction.

He stresses that quality does not mean 'best' but 'best for the customer use and selling price'. Control is seen as a management tool with four steps:

- Setting quality standards;
- Appraising conformance to these standards;
- Acting when the standards are exceeded;
- Planning for improvement in the standards.

Feigenbaum argues that statistical techniques should be employed whenever and wherever they may be useful, but that they are only part of the overall administrative quality control system and not the system itself. The details of the quality programme will be specific for each organization but certain basic areas of attention will be common to all. Total quality control is seen as providing the structure and tools for managing quality so that there is a continuous emphasis throughout the organization on quality leadership.

The need for quality-mindedness throughout all levels is emphasized and the quality control organization is seen as both:

- A channel for communication for product quality information;
- A means of participation in the overall quality programme.

A total quality system is defined by him as:

> The agreed company-wide and plant-wide operating work structure, documented in effective, integrated technical and managerial procedures, for guiding the co-ordinated actions of the people, the machines, and the information of the company and plan in the best and most practical ways to assure customer quality satisfaction and economical costs of quality.

Operating quality costs can be divided into:

- Prevention costs – including quality planning;
- Appraisal costs – including inspection;
- Internal failure costs – including scrap and rework;
- External failure costs – including warranty costs, product recall.

Reductions in operating quality costs result from establishing a total quality system for two reasons:

- Lack of existing effective customer-orientated standards may mean that current product quality is not optimal, given use;
- Expenditure on prevention can lead to a several-fold reduction in internal and external failure costs.

Feigenbaum was founding chair of the International Academy for Quality and is a past president of the American Society for Quality Control, which presented him with the Edwards Medal and the Lancaster Award for his international contributions to quality and productivity. In 1988, he was appointed to the board which oversees the Malcolm Baldrige National Quality Award programme and, in 1991, the fortieth anniversary edition of *Total Quality Control* was published.

Dr Kaoru Ishikawa

Kaoru Ishikawa was born in 1915 and graduated from Tokyo University in 1939 with a degree in applied chemistry. His name will perhaps be best known from the Ishikawa Diagram, otherwise known as the Cause and Effect Diagram or the Fishbone Diagram. Ishikawa invented the diagram (in 1952) to supplement the other tools and techniques that he advocated for the measurement, control and improvement of processes in (mainly) Japanese companies until his death in 1989.

After the war, he returned to Tokyo University and in 1948 began to study statistical methods. By 1949, he had joined JUSE's Quality Control Research Group and, following Deming's visit in 1950, began teaching the application of statistical methods for quality control, making it compulsory for his engineering students at the university.

Ishikawa's contribution to the turnround of Japan's industry since the second world war cannot, perhaps, be overstated. As well as teaching the techniques of quality control directly to all levels within diverse organizations, he pioneered the quality circle movement in Japan, initiated quality conferences, contributed regularly to quality journals and worked closely with the Japanese Industrial Standards Committee which led to him becoming chair of the Japanese Chapter of the International Standards Organization in 1977.

Ishikawa had the rare ability to adopt technical methods, and make them accessible and palatable to all levels within an organization. In particular, he championed the use of what are commonly called the seven tools of quality control:

- Pareto charts – to prioritize action;
- Cause and effect diagrams – to identify causes of variation;
- Stratification – to divide data into subsets;
- Check sheets – for data collection;
- Histograms – to display variation graphically;
- Scatter diagrams – to confirm relationships between two factors;
- Shewhart's control charts and graphs – to monitor and control variation.

The same set of tools was used by teams at all levels and by all functions within organizations for the measurement, evaluation, control and improvement of all business activities, not just for quality control of the product. Furthermore, because the output from the use of the tools is graphical, the information displayed can be understood by all, helping to reduce misunderstandings and obviate communication problems.

Ishikawa's book, *Guide to Quality Control* (Tokyo, Asian Productivity Organization, 1976), based on articles written for the *Quality Control for the Foreman* journal, is a classic text describing the use of these tools. One of Ishikawa's pet themes, highlighted in the book, is the accurate collection and use of data. He argued that all data should be treated with suspicion and historical databases should be ignored. Data should be collected as and where needed.

Company-wide quality

Ishikawa was a key player in the company-wide quality control movement which started in Japan around 1955, following the visits of Deming and Juran. Company-wide quality control necessitates measurement by all. Everyone studies statistical methods. Every function and all levels participate in the improvement process; research, design, engineering, manufacturing, sales, clerical, personnel, etc. Quality control concepts and methods are used to measure, monitor and improve incoming raw materials, manufacturing processes, personnel issues and sales problems. In Ishikawa's concept, quality does not only mean the quality of the product, but also after-sales service, quality of management, the company itself and the human being. As a result, it is argued:

- Product quality improves and becomes uniform. Defects are reduced;
- Product reliability is improved;
- Cost is reduced;
- Productivity increases and it becomes possible to make rational production schedules;
- Wasteful work and rework are reduced;
- Technique is established and improved;

- Expenses for inspection and testing are reduced;
- Contracts between vendor and vendee are rationalized;
- The sales market is enlarged;
- Better relationships are established between departments;
- False data and reports are reduced;
- Discussions are carried out more freely and democratically;
- Meetings are operated more smoothly;
- Repairs and installations of equipment and facilities are done more rationally;
- Human relations are improved.

Quality control circles

Quality control (QC) circles are a major feature of company-wide quality control and illustrate Ishikawa's commitment to education and measurement for all. In 1962 Ishikawa became chair of the editorial board of a low-priced journal entitled *Quality Control for the Foreman*. This was published by JUSE and built on the success of another regular JUSE publication, *Statistical Quality Control*, which originated in 1950. The purpose of the new magazine was to get the message and techniques of quality measurement to the operators in the front line. QC circles began in Japan as study groups – workers and their foremen being encouraged to read and discuss the concepts and methods advocated in *Quality Control for the Foreman*, and then to try the approaches in their own work areas.

The nature and role of circles varies between companies, but the following is a general guide. They typically consist of small groups of five to 10 people from the same work area who meet voluntarily on a regular basis to discuss, investigate, measure and analyze work-related problems. The circle is led by a foreman or one of the workers and the seven tools of quality control are used. Depending on the organization, solutions to problems identified by the circle are either presented to management for authorisation before implementation, or the team has authority to implement directly. Circle members receive no direct financial reward for their improvements.

The aims of the QC circle activities are to:

- Contribute to the improvement and development of the enterprise;
- Respect human relations and build a happy workshop or office offering job satisfaction;
- Deploy human capabilities fully and draw out infinite potential.

The QC circle concept spread rapidly, both within manufacturing companies and also into service organizations. Encouraged by books, seminars, lectures, annual conferences and visits to other organizations, the number of individuals involved in circle activity in Japan is greatly in excess of 10 million. Ishikawa was central to masterminding much of this growth and in laying down the ground rules for circle activities.

Ishikawa is often regarded as the 'father of Japanese quality'. He was awarded the Deming Prize, the Nihon Keizai Press Prize, the Industrial Standardization Prize and the Grant Award. The latter was presented by the American Society for Quality Control in 1971 in recognition for his education programme on quality control. He died in 1989.

Dr Genichi Taguchi and Dr Shigeo Shingo

Taguchi and Shingo are two further Japanese quality gurus whose ideas contributed tremendously to Japan's post-war turnround. Both evolved methods for the prevention of quality problems in manufacture and for the design of efficient processes – but used very different approaches. Over the last decade their methods have been finding increasing application in the West.

Taguchi

Genichi Taguchi was born in Japan in 1924. When the Nippon Telephone and Telegraph Company established its Electrical Communications Laboratory (ECL) in 1949, he was recruited to improve the efficiency of its research and development activities. His first book was published in 1951 and earned him the Deming Award for literature on quality. The book introduced statistical methods for minimizing the number of trials or tests that need to be carried out in order to arrive at a satisfactory design. In 1954–5, Taguchi visited the Indian Statistical Institute where he conducted several experiments, and also met Shewhart and Fisher. Part of Taguchi's methodology is based on the work begun by Fisher in England in the 1920s, but expanded and adapted for industrial applications.

During the 12 years that Taguchi spent with ECL, he consulted widely among many Japanese companies, including Toyota. Like Ishikawa, he was able to simplify complex statistical methods and make them comprehensible to non-statisticians. Taguchi's methods, which in essence build quality into processes and products at the design stage, were therefore available to many Japanese companies from the 1950s. The diagram shown in Figure 3.2 illustrates the relative contributions of the different approaches to quality control used in Japan since the second world war.

Fig 3.2 Relative contributions of quality control approaches in Japan since 1945

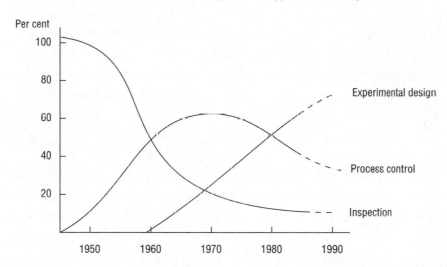

Taguchi methods can be used for trouble-shooting in production, but their main application is in the design of production processes and products. Within a process, the number of factors that contribute to the quality and consistency of the output can be many. Which are the important ones and how important are they? Are they always important or only under certain conditions? To test out and measure the effect of all of the possible combinations of variables and at different levels would be an impossible task. How long can you wait to get a new product to market?

Conventionally, the need to get new products to market quickly can mean that processes are set up based on previous experience, a few trials that nearly worked and with 'fingers crossed' as production starts, in the hope of meeting the agreed deadline. As problems occur, they are dealt with as far as possible by problem solving and at great cost in terms of defectives produced, time wasted, customer dissatisfaction, etc. The process variables are subsequently 'twiddled' in an effort to improve consistency of output and minimize the production of defectives.

Instead, Taguchi's approach uses a standard set of tables to optimize the number of experimental trials that need to be carried out initially. These 'orthogonal arrays' reduce the number of tests dramatically by giving an experimental design pattern which does not measure the effect of every possible combination or level of factors, but gives sufficient measure on each for decisions to be made. Further trials to home in more precisely on the optimum levels can be made if required. As an example of the power of the method: seven different factors each at two levels would require 128 experiments if tackled conventionally; Taguchi uses just eight. For six factors at five levels, equivalent to 625 combinations, Taguchi would carry out 25 experiments initially.

By carrying out the designed experiments, the optimum level and relative importance of each variable is established with regard to the sensitivity of the process to environmental and other uncontrollable factors. Efficient and robust processes can then be set up using these data, and statistical quality control (SQC) and statistical process control (SPC) can be used to monitor and control quality and process characteristics in the critical areas identified.

The 'quality loss function', developed by Taguchi in the early 1970s, may be used to measure and evaluate design decisions on a financial basis. The loss or cost element is defined as 'loss imparted by the product to society from the time the product is shipped'. The loss includes not only the normal company costs of scrap, rework, downtime, warranty, etc but also costs to the customer in terms of poor product performance and reliability, which themselves may result in the manufacturer losing future business. To minimize this loss to society, the variation from the target, for any particular quality characteristic, must also be minimized, usually at extra cost. By using the quality loss function (a mathematical formula), decisions can be made to determine whether additional costs in production will actually prove to be worthwhile in the market place. For this reason, the loss function is usually used at the last phase of designing a new product or process, after the design has already been optimized as fully as possible.

Since 1980, more and more American companies have implemented Taguchi methodology, including Xerox, Ford and ITT. In Europe, with one or two exceptions – such as Lucas – Taguchi's approach found little application until, in 1987, the Institute of Statisticians organized a conference in London to publicize the methods.

Shingo

Born in Japan in 1909, Shigeo Shingo is perhaps not as well known in the West as Ishikawa and Taguchi, although the impact of his work, especially in Japan, has been immense. After graduating in mechanical engineering at Yamanashi Technical College in 1930, he joined the Taipei Railway Factory in Taiwan where he introduced the methods of scientific management. In 1945 he became a professional consultant with the Japan Management Association where, as education department chair in 1951, he first became aware of statistical quality control techniques.

From 1955 he was responsible for industrial engineering and factory improvement training at Toyota Motor Company. In the period between 1956 and 1958, while working at Mitsubishi Heavy Industries in Nagasaki, Shingo was responsible for halving the time for hull assembly of a 65,000 ton supertanker from four months to two months. His methods quickly spread to other Japanese shipyards. In 1959 he left the Japan Management Association and established the Institute of Management Improvement.

From 1961 Shingo started to develop poka-yoke systems. Poka-yoke literally means mistake-proofing and was the name he adopted for the technique after he received complaints for calling the method fool-proofing (baka-yoke). In the West, we often see something of this approach where safety is an issue, but in Japan it is also used extensively where quality is the main concern. Interestingly, poka-yoke systems, by using devices which prevent defects from occurring, obviate the need for measurement. Poka-yoke systems in general involve two phases: the detection aspect and the regulatory aspect. Detection can be accomplished by various means: physical contact, limit switches, photoelectric cells, press-sensitive switches, thermostats, etc. Regulation can be by either giving a warning (e.g., flashing light, alarm buzzer) or by taking control (prevention, automatically shutting a machine down), or both.

Shingo distinguished between 'errors' and 'defects', the latter being caused by the former. He recognized that people do make mistakes, for a variety of reasons, but that errors need not result in defects. His method is to stop the process whenever an error occurs and to establish the source of the error by inspection, and then to prevent its recurrence. Poka-yoke devices, in effect give 100 per cent inspection, but during the process when prevention is possible and not after the event when it is too late. Using Shingo's concept of zero quality control, zero defects can be achieved.

Shingo had been a firm believer in the application of statistical process control since he first learned about it. Gradually, as he did more and more work with poka-yoke systems, his enthusiasm for statistical process control waned. Improvement from statistical methods comes from the detection and measurement of defects and a reaction to them; his methods prevent defects. Furthermore, statistical methods use sampling techniques; his poka-yoke methods allow for 100 per cent inspection and make measurement unnecessary.

By 1977, he was 'finally released from the spell of statistical methods' when a plant in Matsushita's washing machine division had seven months of defect-free operation in its drain-pipe assembly line involving 23 workers producing 30,000 units per month. Since then, many companies have run without producing defects by using Shingo's zero quality control methods.

Poka-yoke systems improve process efficiency, save waste and reduce costs; critical factors for measurement and improvement in any organization. In 1969 while working for Toyota, Shingo developed a system known as single-minute exchange of die or SMED. This improvement methodology similarly reduces waste. The purpose of SMED is to minimize the amount of time taken when making changeovers. It reduces downtime and increases production flexibility, obviating the need for long production runs and large batches. Inventory can be reduced dramatically, because there is less need to maintain stock to cover for the hold-ups.

At Toyota, the set-up time for a 1,000 ton press was four hours, twice as long as it took Volkswagen in Germany. Within six months, Shingo had reduced Toyota's set-up time for the operation to one-and-a-half-hours. Following this initial success, a new target was given – three minutes! Shingo achieved this within three months! Other examples show set-up times being reduced from six hours to six minutes and work-in-progress inventory being slashed by 90 per cent.

Set-up time is made up of two elements which can be measured separately: internal set-up time, when the machine must be stopped, and external set-up time, when the machine need not be stopped. The optimization process involves converting as much internal set-up time to external set-up time, and then relentlessly improving both aspects. The improvements are made by a variety of simplification and de-skilling methods: jigs, clamps, quick-release fastenings, standardization of fittings, etc.

When production hold-ups are reduced dramatically by the application of SMED techniques and when output can be virtually guaranteed by zero-defect production and just-in-time (JIT) operating methods, and Japanese Kanban and production methods become possible. Shingo was a key player in the introduction of these approaches within several companies and Toyota's production system in particular.

Shingo was awarded the Yellow Ribbon Decoration in 1970 for his services in improving production. He wrote more than 14 books, several of which have been translated into English and other European languages. Shigeo Shingo died in 1990.

The early approach to benchmarking
by the Japanese

The first recorded references to the actual physical process of benchmarking itself can be traced to the early 1950s when the Japanese paid visits to Western organizations. Paying particular attention to the manufacturing processes of organizations in the USA and in Western Europe, the Japanese excelled in the absorption of best business practices into their own manufacturing industries; an operation which has effectively resulted in the international reputation of the Japanese in the commercial market.

Benchmarking and the Xerox Corporation

As we discussed in Chapter 1, the Xerox Corporation adopted a vigorous approach to benchmarking in 1979, when it found that competitors were able to sell products more cheaply than Xerox could make them. The approach adopted has now become the model for others to follow. In Robert C. Camp's 1989 book, *Benchmarking: The Search for Industry Best Practices that Lead to Superior Performance* (Milwaukee, ASQC Quality Press, 1989), he cites the definition put forward by David T. Kearns, former CEO of the Xerox Corporation as:

> … the continuous process of measuring products, services and practices against the toughest competitors or those companies recognized as industry leaders.

Today, benchmarking is a key element in business strategy at Xerox. For example, within manufacturing 11 critical parameters have been defined; at the next level, a further 13 have been identified; each of these 24 critical success factors has a benchmark performance against it – what Xerox considers to be the best of the best – and these are continuously updated.

Every aspect of Xerox's business is benchmarked and some of their reported successes in diverse areas are:

- Incoming parts inspection improved to less than five per cent; and quality to 150ppm defects;
- Inventory reduced by two-thirds;
- Engineering drawings per person doubled;
- Marketing productivity improved by one-third;
- Service labour cost reduced by 30 per cent;
- Distribution productivity increased by 8–10 per cent.

An early major benchmarking exercise involved L. L. Bean, the American mail order company and retailer of outdoor clothing. For its warehousing and distribution operation, Xerox identified L. L. Bean as the functional leader to benchmark against, because of its superiority in the areas of order-picking and warehousing. Even though the business area is completely different, the basic operation carried out by the function is very similar.

The Xerox benchmarking process

Xerox has a clearly-defined 10-step process for benchmarking:

- Identify benchmarking subject;
- Identify comparative companies;
- Determine data collection method and collect data;
- Determine current competitive gap;
- Project future performance;
- Communicate findings and gain acceptance;
- Establish functional goals;
- Develop action plans;
- Implement plans and monitor progress;
- Recalibrate benchmark.

In its experience, the area where most people go wrong is at step one. Even within Xerox it is said, there are still people who make site visits and consider that they are carrying out a benchmarking exercise. However, unless the good ideas observed during a visit are in line with the improvement priorities established back at base, there will be little chance of them being implemented. Without a clear definition of what it is that needs changing, without prioritized goals for improvement, any visits are unfocused.

Improvement opportunities are identified by recognizing the critical processes which deliver the critical success factors in the market place. The critical processes are then analyzed and the improvement opportunities identified are prioritized. For example, Xerox has four business pointers as a corporation:

- Customer satisfaction;
- Employee satisfaction;
- Return on assets;
- Market share.

For return on assets, a cause and effect diagram has been used to analyze and give greater understanding of the contributory factors, and how attention should be prioritized for benchmarking activity. Within the marketing group, 10 areas were identified:

- Customer marketing;
- Customer engagement;
- Order fulfilment;
- Product maintenance;
- Billing and collection;
- Financial management;
- Asset management;
- Business management;
- Information technology;
- Human resource management.

Within these 10 areas, 67 sub-processes were identified. Each of the sub-processes became candidates for the improvement process.

Selecting companies to benchmark with

To get information on suitable benchmarking companies, Xerox sub-scribes to the management database, ABI Information. The company also has access to a large technical database. (For more information on databases see Chapter 5.) When searching for someone to benchmark against for its warehousing/distribution operation in 1981, Xerox col-lected and analyzed material from 11 organizations. Databases were consulted, magazines and trade journals covering a three-year period were reviewed, professional associations were asked and consulting firms were contacted.

Although benchmarking is carried out internally and against direct competitors, it is by carrying out functional and generic benchmark-ing that Xerox has identified the greatest improvement opportunities. Xerox used American Express as the benchmark for invoicing pro-cesses, Florida Power and Light for quality management processes, and Ford and Cummins Engines for their factory layout.

Table 3.1

Areas that have been benchmarked	Benchmarking partners
Manufacturing operations	Saturn (a division of General Motors) Fuji-Xerox
Manufacturing safety	DuPont
Factory floor layout	Cummins Engine
Research and product development	Hewlett-Packard
Distribution	L. L. Bean Inc.
Billing and collection	American Express
Quality management	Toyota
Quality improvement	Florida Power and Light
Supplier development	Honda Manufacturing of America

For supplier development, Honda Manufacturing of America has been benchmarked. At the time of the study, Xerox had 10 engineers working with suppliers to improve quality. Honda, meanwhile, a comparative company in terms of costs, had a dedicated supplier development team of 96, over half of whom were graduate engineers!

And this for a key supplier base of 216 for assembled parts, which is somewhat less than the size of Xerox's list of suppliers.

According to Rank Xerox Ltd, the following points are key for successful benchmarking:

- It is essential to understand your own processes thoroughly;
- Visits are not arranged until sufficient desk research has been carried out to ensure that the companies selected are the best that can be found;
- The focus must be on industry best practices;
- There must be a willingness to share information. Reciprocal visits are arranged if required;
- Sensitive information is always kept confidential;
- Getting the process owners or operators to carry out the benchmarking studies is seen as being critical; trying to involve people after the study is too late;
- Do not concentrate on outcomes; it is the practices and processes that need to be understood;
- Benchmarking must be a continuous process; the competition is constantly changing;
- There must be a willingness to change based on the benchmark findings.

Integrating benchmarking within total quality management

Rank Xerox also acknowledges that the incorporation of benchmarking within TQM is not easy. However, some of the problems may be anticipated and thus the impact can be minimized. Accordingly, good practice at Xerox is as follows:

- Tie projects to the corporate goals or priorities. A demonstration of linkage should be inspected and evidence of activities within the planning process should be provided. Do not stray outside the corporate goals and planning process – benchmarking hotels in the

Bahamas may provide some interesting facts, as well as fun, but may not be strictly appropriate;

- Differentiate between competitive analysis and benchmarking. Good applications of a benchmarking process will determine gaps in performance – competitive analysis will give more superficial information;

- Detailed preparation work is required to avoid waste of effort and there are two aspects in particular to consider here. First, bench-marking within the design cycle may be carried out too late and result in a cost-reduction instead of cost-prevention by the intro-duction of cost-effective designs. Second, during the planning pro-cess and the gathering of benchmarking information, there will be a risk of committing manpower and cost in pursuit of wrong tar-gets, metrics or processes. Use visit checklists, etc to ensure focus on the right areas;

- Continuous improvement can be achieved if inspection and encouragement is provided to improve processes, methods and practices. Without this inspection, the roll out and incorporation of benchmarking may falter.

As the first winners of what is now known as the European Business Excellence Award, Bernard Fournier, managing director of Rank Xerox (UK), pointed to benchmarking as a key element of success. Specifically, in his presentation on receiving the Award from King Juan Carlos of Spain in Madrid on October 15, 1992, he described Xerox's use of internal benchmarking as a key element. By 'bench-marking with themselves', sharing best practices with the 22 other Rank Xerox companies in Europe, the company has learned how to combat the 'not invented here syndrome'. Director of quality and cus-tomer satisfaction, Rafael Florez, also described the use of surveys, including an anonymous one asking customers who their top supplier was in a specific target market. Finally, Bernard Fournier concluded by making particular reference to the company's unified health and safety standard and achievements in exceeding the DuPont industry benchmark of five incidents per 200 khrs.

WHAT IT IS ALL ABOUT: THE BENCHMARKING PROCESS

The keys to benchmarking

In previous chapters we have examined the nature of the benchmarking boom and something of the role of benchmarking in the modern world. We have looked at the TQM revolution in management thinking with its focus on internal business processes, and considered the important and revolutionary approach of focusing on such processes in order to identify the potential for improvement. We also considered quality measurement, the need for a unified concept of measurement deployed throughout the organization, the need to measure processes rather than just inputs or outputs and the need for external comparisons. We have also looked at the history of benchmarking, the quality gurus and the history of quality measurement. Finally, we have culminated so far in the Xerox story, a case of benchmarking for survival that shaped the benchmarking boom of today.

To summarize, then, the keys to benchmarking, Western management's move towards TQM has itself represented a natural evolution from naïve ideas of product conformity to specification, often achieved by inspection, through concepts of quality assurance achieved by documentation and control of the processes involved in the production, delivery and management of product or service, to the concept of the self-improving organization. TQM is seen as primarily a management-led approach in which top management commitment is essential.

Key 1: Emphasis on quality

The emphasis is on quality in all aspects and functions of the organization's operation, not just in the provision of a major service or product to the external end customer. Employee awareness and motivation are essential. Employees are responsible for ensuring quality in terms of satisfying the customer in all they do, and the approach is one of prevention of errors and faults rather than detection and correction. Typically, cultural change in the organization from reactive to proactive, and from an inspection to a prevention approach and to one of involvement, is necessary. Organizational change is also typically needed. A strong emphasis is also placed on identifying internal customers and meeting their needs. Emphasis must be placed on supplier–customer relationships. In such programmes, teamwork is often used to ensure involvement and a movement to a continuous improvement culture.

Key 2: Business processes

The second key to benchmarking is the importance of business processes, as identified within most TQM approaches, rather than emphasizing the classical functional divisions of the organization such as finance, stores, sales, etc. The organization is seen as a set of major and minor business processes, each major process being concerned with delivery of a service or product to an end customer and, typically, running across all or many of the functional areas of the organization. Such a process analysis, makes us realize that typically the processes of the business have no single owners and that the end customer has to rely on satisfactory completion of process steps and communication by all the functional areas involved.

By concentrating on the processes instead, we are able to identify process inefficiencies such as delays or queuing at process bottlenecks, lack of control or checking of a crucial process step, situations where the process is itself unable to cope or there is no clear process procedure, and places where responsibility for process activities is not clear. We can identify measurement points in the process, verify how well we are currently doing and plan the introduction of improvements using the measurement points to monitor the improvements being achieved. Concentrating on the process enables us to monitor the internal workings of the system and not just concentrate on the end product that the customer sees which is often too late.

Key 3: The Western TQM model is limited

The third key to benchmarking is the limitation of the TQM model as it has evolved in the West. The crude model concentrates clearly on the need to improve, the importance of the customer, cultural change, of the continuous nature of improvement, on teamwork and on the participation of everyone. While the programme should be steered by top management and the way forward planned, monitored, reviewed and readjusted, the basic data input in this measurement process is often taken naïvely as performance against improvement targets and past performance. While this is a good approach to get started, to break through the cultural barriers created by the mentality of conformance to requirement rather than self-improvement, it itself begs the question as to whether management really has a wide enough view to focus on the improvement process and the real issues. After all, if management accepts the fact that a TQM programme is necessary, it is, in a sense, admitting that its management skills in the past have not been perfect. It is admitting that there is a need to get everyone aligned in the organization to improve, to rethink the organization and the way it does business, to hear the voice of the people that really do the job and the voice of the customers. A caveat of this admission is that management's and the workforce's own conception of what needs to be improved and by how much, might not be as appropriate as it would like to think.

Management can set the priorities against strategic objectives, but it really needs to convince itself that it is not missing anything, that its competitors are not stealing a march on it, that there is not a missing ingredient in the way we do things compared with the way that our competitors do them that really gives them the advantage. And this comparison, of course, is not just limited to our competitors, but to world best practice; on anything we can transfer from another area of activity into that of our own.

Key 4: Systematic external benchmarking

The fourth key to benchmarking is that once we have accepted this need to study our competitors and world best practice, and, also, the importance of internal business processes, then we must bring these two themes together and systematically examine all our internal processes and performance in comparison to external benchmarks. This taxonomy of our internal operations is a necessary requirement for a coherent improvement process.

Key 5: Benchmarking for survival

The fifth and last key to benchmarking is the Xerox story – benchmarking for survival. The experience and expertise Xerox created has contributed enormously to the concept of benchmarking as we know it today. However, it is not, of course, necessary to wait until the last possible moment in the fight for survival to start the process.

Prerequisites

What are the essential prerequisites before we go through the benchmarking process? There can be many problems and pitfalls in benchmarking. Not least are the usual ones encountered when organizations decide to 'implement' the other aspects of TQM.

Commitment from the top is essential if the approach is to be successful and if improvements are to follow from the comparative measuring exercise. Times vary greatly but, generally, initial research activity may take between two and 18 months to complete, and the level of resource that needs to be committed can be very high. Then the hard part, making the improvements, begins. Benchmarking is no quick fix with instant payback; unless senior management shows patience and takes leadership for the change process, the whole activity is likely to become another flavour of the month, resulting in frustration and apathy.

There must be a belief in the need to change. This belief is likely to be reinforced when comparisons with market leaders are made, but it is management's responsibility to generate enthusiasm for improvements and to overcome resistance to change throughout the organization. Benchmarking is a tool to help the change process and not the preserve of a few elite specialists. The people who will be asked to make changes following the benchmarking exercise must be involved with the process from the beginning. Their input will help to prevent silly mistakes being made during the study and they will recognize the need for improvement when the comparisons are made.

If people's introduction to benchmarking comes from the analysis and consists of 'Company X can produce twice as much as you can in half the time', without any reference to *how*, then the reaction is likely to be somewhat different. Not everyone can be part of the investigation team, but it is important to keep people informed of the progress being made by communicating as much information as possible to those who will be involved at the implementation stage.

Benchmarking is a tool for people who are serious about making improvements. Training is necessary, both at the awareness level and for practical application. The benchmarking process needs to be planned, steered, monitored and reviewed if maximum benefits are to accrue and the exercise is not to deteriorate into a 'nice to know' outcome. Trying to do too much too quickly will result in information overload and confused priorities; to allow people to become familiar with the methodology, two or three key areas for investigation are quite sufficient initially. Senior management support and recognition will then act as a spur for further activity.

Planning a benchmarking project

Many organizations which are extremely good at project management on customer projects do not effectively manage their own improvement projects. When under pressure of time, the approach of do it first, and plan it afterwards can be all too common. We all know it does not work, but we do it anyway.

Many TQM and other programmes failed due to inadequate planning and control, or at least never delivered up to their full potential. So to implement benchmarking effectively, we must plan it up-front, clarify and focus the investigation, and its conduct.

How we plan it is more difficult to specify, since our desire to benchmark may have arisen for differing reasons. It may be application-specific, arising from a natural approach to solving a specific problem. It may be instead the result of a general desire to pilot benchmarking as an approach within our organization, or as a next step in TQM.

Whatever the motivation, clearly a written plan will be necessary covering all project stages. These include selection of subject, the internal investigation to clarify current practice and performance, selection of comparative organization(s), collection of external information, analysis and identification of improvement potential, and implementation and validation of improvement. Clearly good planning will require the establishment of a bar chart with milestones and timescales identified.

Selecting the subject

Benchmarking is not about making visits to other companies to try to pick up one or two ideas that may be useful somewhere. Instead, it is centred around planned research arising from a company's recognition that it needs to make improvements in critical business areas. Improvement, generally, is initiated by asking the following:

- Where do we want to be?
- Where are we now?
- What do we need to do to get from here to there?

Any activity that can be measured can be benchmarked, but most organizations will start with those areas where they know they need to be competitive to stay in business. The organization may have a clear mission statement or list of business goals which is used to focus improvement activity. Customer satisfaction is high on most company priority lists, as is the need for a low-cost operation. Deciding these broad areas partly answers the first question above. These broad areas, however, need to be broken down into more specific activities that can be measured. What are the processes that deliver customer satisfaction? What processes eat up the costs? The more precisely you define what you need to measure, the more useful will be the information that you gather to compare it with.

What things are important to customers? What will help them to be successful? How good is the service currently given? What factors cause customer dissatisfaction? An analysis of customer complaints and warranty claims can give some guidance here and, of course, the customer can be asked directly. Questionnaires can be sent out and review workshops can be organized.

Beware of differences in terminology. Reliability of service is a major requirement of most customers, but what does it mean and how is it measured? The answer may be by on-time delivery performance or by levels of defect-free product, or both.

What key measures are already in place to monitor both current performance and the hoped-for improvement? What is your current performance in these areas and what is your current practice for achieving those performances?

The cost of quality approach for identifying areas for improvement is not dealt with in detail in this book, but common areas for benchmarking are the related areas of stock levels, work in progress, waste and reject levels. Again, the cost (measures) for each of these areas should be known, but also it is essential to understand the processes and practices that lead to these costs being incurred. A thorough analysis of what actually happens is necessary, not a blind acceptance of a theoretical process model.

At the end of the exercise, you will need to understand how and why organizations that you have benchmarked have achieved their superiority, not just the levels of attainment that they have achieved. Comparing numbers will not help you to compete; it is necessary to compare the practices that have given rise to the numbers.

Emphasis has been placed on this initial step of selecting the subject because, in our experience and that of leading benchmarking organizations such as Xerox, it is here where most companies get it wrong. Until organizations understand their processes fully and how those processes deliver the current performance in key areas, it is meaningless to make comparisons with other organizations.

When the process is understood, and the critical activities are known and measured, the 'Where are we now?' question will have been answered. It should then be clear where improvements can be made by investigating best practice elsewhere, i.e., the area to be benchmarked. It is essential to make sure, though, that the subjects chosen for benchmarking are based on current market needs and not just on areas that the company considers to be important. In the production of electronic components, for example, a defect-free supply is perhaps now almost taken for granted; the requirements may be instead primarily for service differentiation and time-to-market.

Choosing a comparative organization

Deciding who to benchmark against depends on the subject chosen for benchmarking, the resources that can be made available, and the challenge that an organization is prepared to undertake. In general, there are often seen to be four different types of benchmarking other than product and strategic; each approach has its own advantages and disadvantages.

Internal benchmarking

This involves making comparisons with other parts of the same organization. It can be with other departments, other sites, other companies within the same group, either in the same country or abroad. This type of benchmarking is usually straightforward to arrange and fairly common. It is relatively easy to obtain all of the information necessary for a good comparison to be made. If the operations are similar across the different sites, the data will be instantly relevant and usable, but it is unlikely to yield improvements which meet world best practice.

Competitor benchmarking

This is much more difficult. Any information obtained is likely to be very relevant but, for reasons of confidentiality, it will be almost impossible to get a full picture of how a direct competitor operates. Looking at outputs and available figures can give some information, but they can also mislead if the processes that deliver the outputs cannot be determined. Some of the larger organizations, however, do exchange information in selected areas in the interest of jointly coming to terms with best practice.

Functional benchmarking

This involves making comparisons with typically non-competitor organizations which carry out the same functional activity in which you are interested. Examples are warehousing, procurement, catering, etc. This type of benchmarking has several advantages: functional leaders are easy to identify in many areas; confidentiality is not usually an issue; approaches which may be novel for your industry can be discovered; two-way partnerships can be developed. Weighing against these are likely to be problems in adopting and adapting their practices for your operation.

Generic benchmarking

This goes a step further and may compare business processes which cut across various functions and in quite different industries. Opportunities discovered by this process are likely to be the most innovative and to create breakthroughs for unprecedented improvement. However, the integration of novel concepts into a different industry is also likely to be the most challenging.

The type of benchmarking and organizations chosen to benchmark against depends on many factors. If your organization is large and generally looked on as being a market leader, then the requirement is obviously different from that demanded by a smaller company with perhaps less experience of making quality improvements. The market leader will have a real need to search out best practices, whereas the smaller operator will probably find it easy to identify improvement opportunities by observing the practices of almost any successful company.

Similarly, the level of resource that can be, and needs to be, committed in each case will be different. It makes sense to limit initial visits to local companies if possible; not only will the time and cost be less, but also problems associated with language and cultural differences will be avoided. Obviously, where the opportunity presents itself, internal benchmarking is the ideal place to start. Kodak does this between its various sites, as does Philips. The whole process is relatively easy to manage and gives experience in the technique.

For other types of benchmarking, there are various sources of information which can aid in the identification of organizations to compare against. A simple starting point is the knowledge already within your own company; the marketing function, for example. Then, customers, suppliers and other contacts within the same industry can usually contribute good ideas. Consultants, academics and other industry observers can be asked who they think are the leaders in any particular area. Trade journals, magazines, books and other library material are useful, and ideas can also be picked up at conferences, workshops, and seminars.

One point should be mentioned. How do you know that the company which you have selected for benchmarking really represents the best practice? The answer is that you do not and perhaps never will. If the research you have carried out indicates that it is the best you have yet come across, and their performance is better than yours, then proceed to the next step. Perhaps somewhere there is someone a little better; you may discover them at a later date. It is important to halt the research, temporarily at least, and to start making improvements.

Some companies have sidestepped the issue of whom to benchmark against by opting to use as a benchmark the idealized requirements of the Malcolm Baldrige Quality Award or the European Business Excellence Award. In Japan, companies have prepared themselves for the Deming Award in a similar way, even though the requirements are less clearly defined and structured.

Collecting external information

Although the most valuable information will be obtained by the direct exchange of data with other organizations, much useful material can be gleaned from indirect sources. The sources mentioned in the previous section can be used, supplemented by information from annual reports, public-access databases such as Dialog, research institutes, government agencies, the World Wide Web, etc. However, caution is advised, since some of the data obtained by these means will be out of date or may be wrong for other reasons.

Before descending upon other organizations, it is vital to carry out as much desk research as possible to optimize the value of any visits. To supplement other sources, questionnaires can be prepared and sent to potential benchmark companies, for completion and return before the visit. Also, internal discussions should be held before the visits to establish the extent of current knowledge and to focus the requirements of the investigation so that a comprehensive checklist can be prepared.

Many companies that are not direct competitors are willing to allow access and share information, especially if it will be kept confidential. There will often be a need to sign a non-disclosure agreement. Personal contacts and a professional approach play a major part in opening doors; there is usually a need to convince target organizations that mutual benefit will accrue. Potential benchmarkers should be well briefed and be given sufficient authority to trade sensitive information. Often, a partnership for the exchange of data develops, with reciprocal visits and regular meetings to compare notes.

Independent bodies can be used to gather data from competitive companies, but here it is often only the numbers that can be obtained and not the processes that deliver the numbers. Independent go-betweens, such as consultants and academics, can also blind sensitive data from competitors.

Analyzing the data and implementing improvement

The data from benchmarking exercises will obviously differ depending on the activity that has been investigated. However, it should be made up of two elements:

- What is achieved in terms of numbers (*the performance metrics*);
- How and why it is achieved (*the practice*).

Neither of these is of much use without the other. These two sets of data need to be considered and compared with your current performance in the same area. A further consideration may well be the difficulty of transferring a process that works well in one endeavour into a completely different industry. The questions are as follows:

- How big is the gap between your performance and theirs?
- How much of their experience is applicable to your situation?

If the data collected during the study is directly comparable, the performance gap is instantly meaningful. Even if your performance is superior, there may be things to learn from what others do. The main lessons, though, come from studies which show that your performance is inferior. The question of 'Where do we want to be?' can now be answered in detail, with quantified goals based on a knowledge of what the leaders are achieving and how. If the processes, products, company size or business areas are not very similar, then the interpretation of the data will be more difficult and the performance gap may not be as meaningful.

It may also be more difficult to answer: How do we get from here to there? What can be done to close the gap? How can the positions be reversed, bearing in mind that your competitors are also making improvements and trying to widen the gap? How far will you go to adopt and adapt new practices? What is involved, how much will it cost and how long will it take? What are the broader implications for the company? These are issues that need to be tackled by teams, involving those who really understand the current practices, those with responsibility for steering the future of the company and those with the authority to make the changes.

Once the decision is made to proceed, implementation of the changes must be planned and steered. New targets for the critical activity can be set, based on the benchmark data, and good leadership will be essential to maintain focus and prevent backsliding. Progress toward the new objectives will need to be reviewed regularly and senior management will have a key role to play in overseeing and providing support for the whole implementation process.

Successful companies have taken on board the fact that improvement is a never-ending journey. A commitment to benchmarking as a driver for continuous improvement means that the implementation of a change to current practices is the end of the beginning, not the beginning of the end.

Nothing stands still and as soon as a new practice is established or a benchmark performance is reached, it may already be out of date. If the activity is still considered to be central to the organization's existence, it is necessary constantly to review the benchmark for that activity and repeat the process of looking for best practice wherever it can be found. Xerox calls this stage 'recalibrating the benchmark'.

Chapter

DATABASES

5

Introduction

During the benchmarking study two types of information will be collected. These are primary and secondary sources. Primary sources of information are obtained directly from the benchmarking partner(s), or target; whilst information about potential benchmarking targets and best practice(s) can be obtained from a variety of secondary sources. Useful information can be gathered from employees, customers, suppliers, academics, librarians, conferences and publications. Typically, such secondary sources of information can be found in the public domain as illustrated by a benchmarking survey in the UK undertaken jointly by Coopers & Lybrand and the CBI in 1994. According to this survey almost 100 per cent of respondents claimed to be using 'published external data'.

Historically, the search for benchmarking partners and best practice information proved to be time-consuming and complex. Back in 1981, it took the Xerox Corporation 10 months to undertake the initial acquisition and assessment of information before an appropriate benchmarking partner was even identified. The situation has now dramatically changed. Since the advent of electronic retrieval, the information-gathering stage has the ability to be speeded up considerably.

Electronically-retrievable information

Robert Camp and Bjorn Anderson's benchmarking survey undertaken in 1995 indicated that the use and benefits from online databases for a benchmarking study were likely to increase. Consistent with these findings is the emergence of an amazing array of databases. There are now according to one source, more than 10 billion database records held in 10,033 major online databases or files, of which 3,014 have been categorized broadly as 'business' in their coverage. These are produced by 2,938 database producers and made available to online users by 1,805 database hosts.

Databases and benchmarking

The potential of databases for benchmarking studies is significant. Three obvious areas are:

- Identification of a potential best practice partner together with information surrounding the area of best practice;
- Where a best practice partner has already been identified, to access 'extra' information that is required to further determine the suitability of the partner;
- To determine performance measurement in terms of comparative business economic/financial data.

When it comes to identifying where an organization is an exemplar of best practice in a particular area, there is a high probability that information about it will have been captured on the many 'business' databases, such as ABI/Inform, Management Contents, Dunn & Bradstreet and the like.

In respect of obtaining extra information on an already-identified best practice partner, among the many databases that can be accessed for extra organizational information are *ICC British Company Financial Datasheets* and *Kompass Europe*. ICC provides information centred around 205,000 British companies including; company name and address, directors' names, etc. *Kompass Europe* provides business information on over 300,000 European companies.

Finally, since benchmarking helps to improve process efficiency and by so doing cuts costs, this factor may be determined by the company's overall performance as illustrated by financial data. Many databases contain both current and historic data on various financial aspects of organizations. Such information could therefore be used to determine performance measurement on a competitive analysis basis. For example, ICC British Company Financial Datasheets contain four-year runs of 70 items of such information for about 205,000 UK companies.

Selecting an appropriate database

The world's largest host system is the Dialog service which has access to over 450 databases. The databases represent a wide range of disciplines and offer full-text trade journals, newspapers, newswires, patents, demographic data and information on companies. In particular the Dialog service is noted for its collection of business information. One of the databases that the Dialog service is host to can be particularly helpful in locating information in respect of potential best-practice partners. The ABI/Inform database is one of the oldest and largest electronic sources of business information. It contains more than 500,000 citations that provide complete bibliographic information and abstracts from selected full-text articles from more than 1,000 business journals. More than 350 are international journals that provide business news and analysis from around the world. More importantly, this information is reasonably current in that the database is updated weekly.

A database such as ABI/Inform is frequently used for benchmarking studies. This is available through at least 14 different hosts, which can make selection difficult. Factors that should be taken into consideration are:

- The range of databases provided by any particular host;
- Whether your organization's future information requirements are going to vary;
- Resources in terms of time and cost.

An obvious advantage of using a large host, such as Dialog, is that the system offers a broad range of databases, so that the database can be used for purposes other than benchmarking.

Overview of online database charges

An explanation of potential changes is given in Table 5.1. However, costs can differ according to the type of database that is being used and the cost of searches which are undertaken by the inexperienced may be quite high because searching for benchmarking data can prove to be complex. The underlying advantage of using an online database is that the time taken to conduct desk research is reduced. Databases can help identify potential targets, extra information about partners and best practice areas.

Table 5.1

Potential charges	Explanation
Subscription charges	Often required on either an annual or monthly basis. Discount plans might be available
Connect time charges	These are different for each database searched. Sometimes discounts are offered where usage exceeds a particular amount
Screen display/print charges	Sometimes there is a separate tariff for online and offline prints. Typically, however, offline prints are more expensive. Immediate delivery is sometimes available by fax but this can also prove to be expensive
Telecommunication charges	Since access is increasingly via the host's dedicated network or through the Internet, these will often be no more than the cost of a local call
Session rate	This is a rate charged per session between log-on and log-off. These are not commonly charged

Where an organization does not, however, subscribe to an online database, a library may have relevant databases on CD-Rom or offer online access. In addition, a university librarian, an academic or information broker could also prove useful. However, it should be remembered that someone else searching on your behalf will need a thorough briefing.

The Internet

Over the past couple of years more and more useful information about benchmarking is being provided on the Internet. Various institutions promoting the use of benchmarking within organizations frequently offer their services via their own web sites. Useful benchmarking web addresses can be found in Table 5.2.

Table 5.2

Web address	Description
http://www.benchmarking.org	Benchmarking Exchange
http://www.ozemail.com.au/~benchmrk/	Benchmarking in Australia
http://www.benchmarking.co.uk/centre.htm	Benchmarking Centre Limited (UK)
http://www.apqc.org/	American Productivity and Quality Center
http://www.va.gov/fedsbest/index.htm	US Inter-Agency Benchmarking and Best Practices Council
http://www.aqc.org	Australian Quality Council Benchmarking Edge

The Benchmarking Exchange

One institution that makes use of the Internet as a means of providing information on potential best practice partners is the Californian-based Benchmarking Exchange (TBE). TBE gives contacts in organizations interested in benchmarking different processes. TBE provides an electronic bulletin board on the Internet to help those seeking benchmarking partners.

Extracts of an Internet search are shown in Figure 5.1. These relate to organizations that were interested in benchmarking their warehousing activities. They have been rendered anonymous and are reproduced from TBE's partnering position board.

Fig 5.1 Results of search using TBE bulletin board

Company A is interested in talking to those who have a warehouse operation that 'picks' small items or supplies. We are interested in metrics on: percentage of orders pulled; wrong materials selected; labelling processes; mislabelling; and similar processes in the warehousing and distribution of materials.

Company B is interested in identifying companies willing to exchange measured information regarding their warehousing distribution operations. Specifically we are interested in production, quality, cost and timing measurement results. Company B operates in a 'piece pick', 'pick to tote', or 'pick to light' type of distribution environment. If you are interested in participating with us, or can suggest companies that might have an interest please respond via TBE or phone …

Company C is benchmarking some of its warehousing activity. We are looking for cost information on the warehousing function. For example: total cost of warehousing per square foot of space, per unit, per man hour, per dollar value of inventory. If you would like to share information or participate in the benchmark, please contact Company C or respond through TBE.

Organizations that believe it would be beneficial to join TBE pay an annual subscription, but do not pay for the costs of any searches, as is the case of the Dialog system.

INTERNAL BENCHMARKING

The current position and potential for internal benchmarking

In Chapter 4, we defined internal benchmarking as essentially the process of making comparisons with other parts of the same organization. This is a loose definition, since comparisons could be with other departments, other sites, other companies within the same group (either in the same country or abroad) or between workteams even within the same department. In this chapter we shall explore all of these possibilities. We shall look, in particular, at the potential for exploiting benchmarking within a group of companies and making comparisons between and within departments, and at mechanisms for benchmarking of workteam and individual performance.

It is, in many senses, remarkable that such internal benchmarking is not already a way of life. It is hard to believe that group management does not bring together the experience and best practice within a group to assist the performance and development of all parts of the organization. Yet it is abundantly clear that in most Western groups this does not happen. Group structures and the power of the centre tend to vary, but on the whole group companies tend to be responsible to the centre only for financial performance. As long as targets are met, or performance is not too disastrous, individual local companies are left very much to themselves.

Even if contact exists with the centre, very often individual managers or engineers are not in direct contact with their opposite numbers in other locations. The limited contact that does exist takes place on either a formal route or informal route. Formal routes may include annual, six-monthly or quarterly meetings. They tend to have a centrally determined format or agenda, to deal with aspects of performance (outputs) or of central policy (inputs), as well as perhaps attempting to assist in the process of introduction of new technology, or similar. Informal links arise often because of career movements between corporate sites and tend to provide a means for individual managers to make contact with some source of knowledge or experience about a particular relevant subject. The very informality of these relationships, however, mitigates against a strong analytic approach and represents more the transfer of 'gut feel' based on individual experiences between individuals at various sites, who themselves may be very isolated.

Thus both formal and informal links, which exist within most corporate groups at present, are not ideal as the exemplars of the benchmarking principles.

Exploiting the potential of the group

The group, however, has enormous potential in this area of sharing best practice, providing benchmarks, and comparative measures of achievement. For this to happen, however, there does need to be a belief that a systematic advantage can be obtained by all participants. All too often, attempts at convening such best practice forums within groups by the centre, are seen by the operating companies as 'interference from head office and the corporate seagulls'. While a site may be under an obligation to participate in such programmes, no real benefit may be anticipated.

Where the establishment of self-improvement forums arises as a direct result of personnel at various operating companies getting together, this is typically hampered by a concern about lack of interest from group, or even hostility, and therefore a lack of support from other senior managers at the various sites.

How then, to do it right? The reality is that in many groups this type of activity has never been planned and policy at the centre is not always clear. Accordingly, one sees short spells of interest by senior central managers leading to the formation or development of such forums, but since there is no established, long-term policy on their role and the place for internal benchmarking, personnel changes and career progression often bring such programmes to a screeching halt, or a more gradual decline.

One key to doing it right then is *planning*. An important aspect of this is the development of clear objectives for the benchmarking activity and a clear view of its priority. The central board must see the need for the activity, to ensure that best practice spreads more quickly among its various operating companies. This belief in its importance by the central board, as well as what it can do for the individual companies, must be communicated effectively to the senior management of the operating companies in a way that it becomes a clear priority for their own operation. As always with benchmarking, however, there is only limited advantage in identifying and evaluating best practice if there is not a clear will, both at the central level and at the operating company level, to then introduce best practice into other sites.

The mechanism for the spread of best practice is also problematical. Central collection of information tends to be regarded by the operating companies as restrictive, rather than as the basis for enabling transfer of best practice. The threat of central interference, or even sale, has frequently come to the fore in the minds of the managers of the operating companies.

In consequence many groups, including a number of those operating a 'lean central' model, have instead concentrated on a central enabling role. A central unit under the direct control of a central board director provides, or offers (sometimes on a contract basis), a support service to the operating companies. Here again though, frequently the emphasis is on the provision of the expertise at the centre to the operating companies rather than on the sharing of best practice between the operating companies. This, therefore, frequently results in a feeling in the operating companies that the central function is irrelevant, perhaps staffed with personnel who have insufficient experience of the real world and their actual situation, and that, 'as always', they have to deal with their real problems themselves. In many cases, it has also been true that there is an element of validity in these accusations.

Given the above dangers, clearly the right way forward is a combination of ownership by the operating companies and by the group centre. To facilitate such ownership and to make the internal benchmarking network a reality, champions are needed in each of the operating companies and again in the centre. Drive from the centre is very attractive, but it must be an enlightened drive facilitating the discussion and comparisons between operating companies, rather than prescriptively instituting solutions.

Clearly, in a large group, it will not be possible to identify champions and make benchmarking a clear priority simultaneously in all the operating companies, nor probably would this be desirable. Some companies will have more immediate time- and energy-consuming activities that they must complete; such as introducing a new technology or obtaining certification to ISO 9000, etc. In most cases, operating companies will be self-selecting, although subject to the encouragement of the champion at the centre. This may well mean that the best companies in the group, the ones that potentially have least to gain from benchmarking with other group companies, will be the first to sign up. While this may seem far from ideal, it does provide probably the best basis for the internal benchmarking forum to get off the ground, since the people involved will be the most informed, the most motivated and from the companies best able to take the long-term view. The forum will therefore be in its best position to survive the initial problems of start-up, to get round management indifference or hostility, to survive changes in personnel at the centre and in the operating companies, or even changes of corporate policy. With this strength, aided by the corporate champion, new member sites or operating companies can be introduced to the forum activities.

To begin with, such activities may be relatively simple; meetings held at each other's sites, with presentations of local approaches and performance, as well as, perhaps, workshop sessions on fundamental concerns across group companies. This can form the basis for individual or small group benchmarking partnerships between member companies. The whole forum may develop a benchmarking grid, and set up crucial measures against which to measure themselves and each other. As time passes, the forum as a whole may begin to engage in collective external benchmarking, selecting world best practice companies outside the group for comparison. Again, the pooled resources thus available and the collective weight of the consortium may facilitate such external benchmarking, when it might be prohibitive for an individual member company.

The organization of such a forum typically requires some resources and a secretariat. Frequently, these are provided by the centre. If, as in some groups, there is a management consultancy, research or training facility in the group which is itself run as an operating company, then this may play host at least part of the time to the group and provide the secretariat, possibly based on a straightforward membership fee. The group-wide forum concept has many advantages over the one-off service from a central facility and also over the concept of participation in external multi-organization clubs. Continuity is provided, with a reduction in the problems of commercial confidentiality, to some extent shared circumstances and reinforcement of some already existing personal relationships.

Mechanisms for inter- and intra-departmental comparisons

The same advantages which exist for internal benchmarking of operating companies within the group also apply for inter-departmental benchmarking and even comparisions within a department. Different departments may possess similar functional activities, or business processes, or may have common aspects of work organization or personnel matters. For example, each department may have to work out its holiday rota, deal with its inter-departmental and external mail each morning, organize its own secretarial work and handle incoming messages when relevant staff are not available. Benchmarking of these working practices, organizational issues and the corresponding successful performance against other departments can be highly beneficial, leading to the spread of best practice identified in one part of the organization to other departments.

It is interesting that this aspect of internal benchmarking has only rarely been labelled as a benchmarking activity, despite its clear similarity to the processes described in the previous section.

The spreading of good practice from one department to another is in fact a problematic area. In most organizations the 'not invented here syndrome', together with inter-departmental communication barriers, mean that such good practice is unlikely to spread, unless identified at a sufficiently senior level of management and consciously legislated for, or encouraged, throughout more departments.

For organizations pursuing quality improvement or TQM programmes, a further complication is the need to balance local involvement, identification and development of solutions, with the need to spread good practice as quickly as possible. In the real world, many TQM programmes are particulary deficient in this respect, since the spreading of good practice identified at a local level has not been clearly thought through. To be consistent with the objectives of TQM, each local area needs to evaluate the worth and transferability of the 'superior' practice developed elsewhere, decide positively to pursue its introduction and gain clear ownership of its implementation. This is in contrast to central management legislating for its introduction and is completely consistent with the concept of benchmarking.

Typically, the same problems which exist at the group level of benchmarking exist also at the inter-departmental level. In particular, the role of central management in relation to departmental management is crucial. The primary need is for a facilitation role, with the ownership of the process of searching for better practice being with the local departmental management. Central management can be key in getting departments, or departmental representatives, together in exactly the same way as corporate management may do for group operating companies.

There are, however, advantages at this inter-departmental level compared to that at group level. Typically, central management is much more in control. Communication between departments, however bad, is better, as is communication with central management. Staff are much more likely to know each other and already to have to work together in certain respects. Perhaps more importantly, the TQM programme is concentrating on involving everyone, and staff are participating not just within their departments but across departmental boundaries. Thus the culture is appropriate to this particular internal benchmarking process. In addition, the steering group of senior management heading up the site TQM programme, as well as the facilitators supporting the programme, are in an excellent position to identify good practice, and encourage its investigation and transfer.

Unfortunately, since most TQM programmes focus in greatest detail at the site or operating company level rather than at group level, there is no analogue of these mechanisms at the level of group benchmarking.

How a department sets about benchmarking itself against others varies, largely according to the nature of the TQM programme introduced. Where, as in most successful programmes, responsibility for quality improvement is placed on departmental management early (so there is no separation into quality and 'real work'), then part of the department's planning should specifically identify opportunities for learning from other departments. Included in this will be the straightforward transfer of practices, as well as the broader use of information from other departments to solve local problems. The important message here is that for this type of activity to succeed, there must be a coherent approach to departmental improvement, as well as the inter-functional, inter-departmental improvement teams which are often highlighted, perhaps too greatly, within TQM programmes.

All that has been said at the inter-departmental level can be repeated at lower levels within departments. Ultimately, successful work teams or quality circles can benchmark aspects of their activities against those of others. Indeed, it is noteworthy that many successful quality circle programmes do encourage healthy competition between circles. This in itself provides motivation.

CASE STUDY: Inter-group benchmarking at GPT Payphone Systems

Comments

As part of the post graduate courses in quality and business management run by the Quality Unit at Nottingham Trent University, students are required to conduct a benchmarking study. This account of an inter-group benchmarking study conducted by two former students based at GPT Payphone Systems highlights the significance of internal benchmarking within a limited timescale and also reflects some of the points made in this chapter.

Introduction

GPT Payphone Systems manufactures payphones, cards (phone cards, smart-cards, etc) and payphone management systems. It has a wide customer base, selling to more than 100 customers in 80 countries. Just as in most companies, GPT is seeking to improve continually its operations and processes.

To make the most of the benchmarking study, senior management at the Chorley site were given an overview of benchmarking to not only expand their understanding, but also to gain their commitment and harness their suggestions as to which process should be chosen. To help us understand where to focus our efforts we had to ask ourselves a couple of important questions. These were:

- What would make a big improvement in our relationship with our customers?

- What would make the most significant improvements in our bottom line?

Taking into account the limited time for the study, a decision was made to look at the customer returns process in respect of a major customer, where a specific problem existed regarding length of turnround times. This was particularly important to the customer. At a management meeting it was pointed out that another GPT company, Public Networks Group (PNG), had a long and successful working relationship in this respect with this customer and could prove to be an ideal inter-group benchmarking partner. It was also mentioned that another student worked for PNG and was closely involved in the customer returns process. At this point it was agreed that PNG would make an ideal internal benchmarking partner. By choosing another GPT company, we would be comparing fairly similar operations so that their experience would be directly relevant and it would be reasonably easy to access information. In addition, from a legal point of view, we were able to exchange information without breaking UK or European Community law.

The benchmarking study: a plan of action

The first act was to draw up a plan of action to meet the limited timescale. Consideration was given to the information that would be required, how it would be accessed and analyzed. It was decided that a visit would be the best method and based on this and other information a project action plan was drawn up (Figure 6.1). The first two points on the action plan had already been decided at a management meeting. The real tasks of obtaining information and how it would be used was still to be done.

Fig 6.1 Action plan

1. Decide what to benchmark

2. Identify benchmarking partners

3. Establish contacts

4. Review and fully understand our own customer returns process

5. Visit PNG to view and fully understand their customer returns process and to gather data on specific activities and then establish performance measures

6. Compare data

7. Feedback of performance measures to senior management to decide on actions

8. Produce report and prepare for presentation

9. Present report

The validity of PNG as a benchmarking partner

After the management meeting where it was suggested that PNG would be a suitable partner, initial research was carried out through contacts at PNG, to establish if the process appeared to be comparable and whether performance was better. Responses suggested that the PNG process was similar, that performance was good and customer satisfaction high. Contact was therefore made with the colleague at PNG who agreed to a visit being made.

Understanding the customer returns process

Before we could contemplate comparing the returns processes, it was imperative that we fully understood our own. The easiest way to do this was to produce a process deployment flowchart (Figure 6.2) which detailed the cast of characters involved. It also showed the negative paths which could add cost or delay. This flowchart was completed with the help of the payphone service centre manager, a key representative of the process owners.

The whole of the process was then reviewed from start to finish looking at factors such as:

- Backlog of items waiting to be booked in;
- Methods used to book items in;
- Methods used to inspect and test items;
- Interface with other departments;

- Time taken to return items to customers;
- Amount of items returned as a percentage of delivery;
- What documented procedures were in place and whether they were being adhered to;
- Strengths and weaknesses of the department.

From this information, it was decided to use the following as performance measures in the benchmarking exercise with PNG:

1. Backlog waiting to be booked in, in days.
2. In-process time, in days.
3. Total turnround time, in days.

Visit to benchmarking partner

Contact was made with the colleague at PNG who arranged for a visit to be made to review their customer returns process. In advance of that visit the nature of the project and the information needed was explained, together with the degree of detail that was desired. It was also explained that all information received would be treated in confidence. Because Payphone Systems and PNG were both GPT companies, it was soon established that there was no problem with either the visit or the information requested.

It soon became evident from research and the visit, that PNG was better at handling customer returns – the booking-in methods were much faster and items were turned around faster.

Comparing the data and the process

Table 6.1 compares the main findings and shows performance gaps needing to be addressed. It was noted that PNG used a buffer stock (a pre-determined quantity of items held in readiness) from which they could send a replacement, immediately if required). Payphone Systems used no such buffer stock, so any problems led to delays.

Fig 6.2 Flowchart for the customer returns process at GPT Payphone Systems

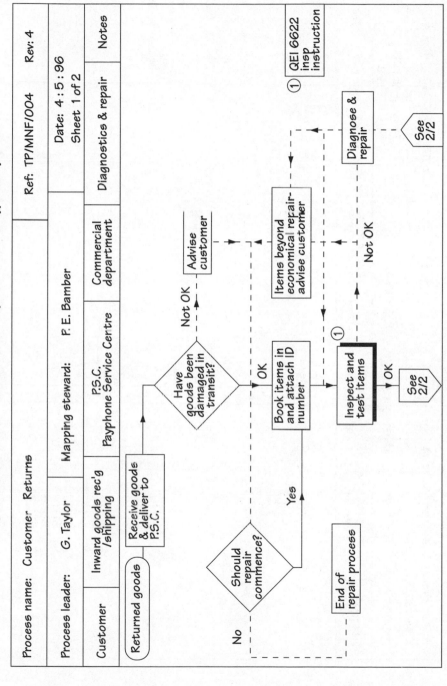

Fig 6.2 (Continued)

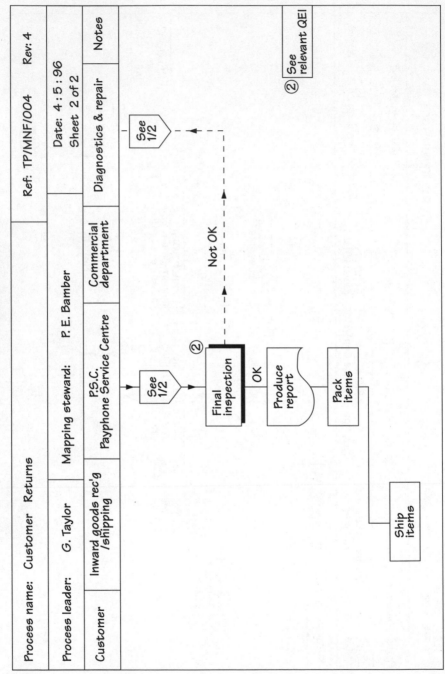

Table 6.1

Measure	Payphone Systems	PNG
Backlog waiting time	1–3.5 days	No backlog
Booking-in method	Fill in paper form and manually enter on computer systems	Swipe bar code labels
Booking-in time	Paper from: 5–10 min Computer: 2–2 min Total average: 10 min	0.75 min
In-process time	Average: 9 days	93% in 4 days 100% in 7 days
Total turnround	2 days to book 9 days to process Average 11 days total	As in-process time
Use of buffer stock	No	Yes

In addition, the way information on each item was recorded and entered onto the computer system was significantly different. In Payphone Systems information was first filled in on a paper form, a copy of which went through the process with the item. From this form the data was entered onto the computer system. However, there was often a delay. As the item moved through the process, various details were entered onto the accompanying form. Only at the end was this data entered onto the computer system, again after a delay. The result was that the system never provided accurate live information and could not be used to track items. In comparison, PNG read in the data at each stage using bar codes, so the computer data was always live and showed exactly where each item was.

Each business produces reports from the computer system detailing monthly returns, items cleared, fault analysis, etc which appeared to be satisfactory to both the management and the customer. However, the Payphone Systems reports could not be as accurate as those in PNG.

Presenting the findings

Having carried out the benchmarking exercise and analyzed the data, it was time to present the findings and secure some level of agreement and commitment to implement appropriate improvements.

The findings were presented and received with great interest. There was particular enthusiasm for using bar code labels for tracking items through the shop floor manufacturing process.

It was agreed that the cost and effort to implement bar code swiping to book in returns would be insignificant (the cost of a bar code reader and installation being £300). It would result in a saving of nine minutes per item, equivalent to £3 per item standard cost and a reduction in the two-day back-log booking-in time. Booking in just 100 items would pay for it. The payphone service manager was asked to implement this as a top priority. It was also agreed to investigate the possibility of using bar code tracking throughout the customer returns process, because this offered superior live information from the system, together with more effective expediting.

Initially there was some resistance to holding buffer stocks with the following issues being raised:

- Lack of space in the payphone service centre;
- Cost of holding the stock of modules;
- The many different items compared with PNG's few;
- The impact of engineering change orders.

However, after a good deal of discussion, it was agreed that a small buffer stock of the main modules would be held, and if this proved to be beneficial in terms of customer satisfaction and cost, then extending it would be considered.

Regarding the monthly reporting from the system, it was agreed that this was generally satisfactory, with the acknowledgement that more accuracy would result should bar code tracking be introduced.

It was noted that if the backlog of two days could be eliminated, more effective expediting could then be expected to reduce average turnround from 11 days to six.

The payphone service manager was to monitor and measure the improvement due to the new procedures. Subsequent follow-up meetings were set up to review the implementation plan and the results achieved.

Conclusions

The inter-company benchmarking study on customer returns proved to be very beneficial in terms of identifying areas where real improvements could be made. The results were welcomed by the management team with their commitment being gained to implement improvements.

GPT Payphone Systems has now implemented the bar code booking-in system and the number of items booked in during one day has risen from 80 to over 300. This reduced the backlog to less than one day and average turnround times dropped from 11 to nine days. This also ensured that the information held on the computer is current and 'live', so traceability has been greatly improved (there was always a chance that the hard copy record sheet could be lost in transit). The whole point of the study was to achieve improvement and we are already seeing improvements in the process.

In view of the opportunities for improvement that the benchmarking study highlighted, GPT Payphones Systems went on to develop further the ideas of bar code booking and tracking and small buffer stocks into an advanced replacement service. This provided next-day delivery of replacements for returned items to support 3,000 payphones as a trial. A success rate of 99.7 per cent was achieved, prompting a letter of commendation from the customer. The bar coding achieved same-day booking-in and was also developed to provide complete tracking of items through the repair process, together with fault analysis for use in product improvement.

Peter Bamber (formerly of GPT Payphone Systems)
Phil Roughley (GPT Payphone Systems)

EXTERNAL BENCHMARKING AND HOW TO DO IT

Selecting comparative organizations

How do we select an organization against which to compare ourselves, our process, our function, even our products? The answer is that there is not one method but several. Which is applicable will depend on your particular subject and circumstances. Selection can be based on knowledge already within your own organization, initial screening surveys, database keyword searches, networking, personal interviews, telephone interviews, review of media reports, direct observation, company publications, awards and accolades, public reputation, or public presentations, or anything else. Three points, however, are crucial:

- Considerable disciplined desk research needs to be done as part of the process of selecting the organization for the external investigation. We must be very sure that the organization or organizations have been selected as appropriate for a specific benchmarking comparison; that they are the most appropriate and that we do have a reasonable prospect of obtaining the information we require about them.

- Plan the conduct of the external investigation and conduct it carefully, rather than just let it happen. The planning itself depends on the outcome of the internal investigation, in which we have identified key areas for comparison and improvement, as well as contacts, budget, and resources available.

- We must behave legally and ethically, and this must also be consistent with our own company or organizational policy.

Finding out about them

To some extent, the same methodology may be used to find out about the selected organizations, as to identify them in the first place. In most cases this will be done directly. Direct contact with the selected organization can be established and discussions, data exchanges, and visits can be organized. Alternatively, at the other extreme, all information may have to be obtained from indirect sources, as in many cases of competitor benchmarking.

Even if direct contact is to be established, and possibly a partnership relationship is to be set up, it is crucial to first fully investigate relevant information about the target organization using indirect sources, so as to clarify the issues, confirm your selection, and show yourselves to be professional and focused when you do make direct contact. Related approaches that will come in useful include classic desk research techniques, using in-house (non-confidential) and general publications, public domain databases, Press and media reports, information about awards and accolades won, as well as conference and seminar presentations.

Also important will be various forms of informal, and possibly formal, interview and questionnaire techniques, applied both to employees of the target organization and third parties (such as industry experts). If the selection and investigation of comparative organizations needs to be done in stages, a survey of likely targets may be necessary, and this can be done in a similar way.

Telephone interviews, personal interviews, and mail, fax or electronic mail questionnaires all have their relative merits. The first two approaches do have the advantage of providing an opportunity to establish personal relationship and rapport, but to do this it may be better to make the interview, by telephone in particular, very informal. Nevertheless, a list of prepared questions should be constructed (and reviewed) prior to commencing. We need, as always, to be sure what we want to know. Of course, it is also important to be sure to whom you are talking and that he or she is the right person. Telephone interviews have the advantage of allowing data to be gathered very quickly while still allowing you to establish an opening for further face-to-face discussion.

Although direct conversation with third parties or employees of target organizations is a rich source of information, it is important to remember that such people can act as filters or distorters of the real facts. This may be accidental or deliberate. They may tell you the corporate line, describing processes and practices in glowing terms, omitting problems and failures, or they may just tell you what you want to hear. We need to be very careful how we question them, by not leading them to answers, not being too aggressive, and by looking always for evidence and corroboration.

With well-designed mail, fax or electronic mail surveys, *potentially* you can get a lot of information very quickly. The chief disadvantage, however, is that you have little control over who responds or, indeed, if they will respond at all. Xerox quotes a response rate of 30 per cent to 40 per cent as being very good, but typically may be much lower.

The design of surveys and interview questions, for brevity, ease of completion, layout, format, clarity, etc is crucial. If you use this method, get some professional help if possible.

The choice of interviewee is an interesting question. Often the assumption is that your direct counterpart in the benchmark organization or in your relevant area will be the best subject. This may be the case, but do not overlook knowledgeable resources elsewhere in the organization or outside. Vendors and suppliers, industry experts, and consultants are all potentially good sources of information.

As well as interview-based methods, there is, of course, also direct observation. This will be particularly appropriate during benchmarking visits, as discussed later. People do not always know how they do things, know how to explain them, or understand what you are asking. If, however, you can see them as they are, or as it is happening, you yourself will be able to ascertain method and relevance.

Related to direct observation, is the potentially thorny issue of reverse engineering. This can be extremely useful for product benchmarking, but also for finding out about manufacturing and assembly processes. It involves acquiring, usually by purchasing, a competitor's product and taking it apart piece by piece to determine how each part was designed, manufactured, and assembled. However, be careful to ensure this is legal.

Xerox points out that the idea of reverse engineering can also be applied in a non-engineering or service process, such as telephone answering, but once again, be careful of the legal issues.

Being ethical

Some of the legal issues of benchmarking are discussed in Chapter 11. Carrying out the external investigation is a key stage, where, by the nature of the activities, we need to be very careful that what we are doing is legal. If we follow one of the mainstream benchmarking codes of conduct, this is likely to be the case and, in addition, we are likely to be acting ethically also, hence ensuring that others will want to continue to co-operate with us.

There are, however, some dubious practices which are not part of real benchmarking that we need to beware. Since legal systems vary, the exact position also varies, but generally the following will be illegal activities:

- Phoney bids: do not ask a customer to falsely solicit bids from another company to enable you to gain competitive information;

- Conditions on suppliers: while you may ask suppliers for competitor's volume figures, do not make divulging that information a condition of doing business;

- Reverse engineering: make sure that the product has been obtained legally, and watch out for design and copyright issues if you build your own version;

- Photography: covert photography, including aerial photography, is unlawful;

- Requesting proprietary information: beware of discussing pricing, for example, or asking for price lists since it can look like collusion and price fixing.

In addition, the following activities are dubious ethically and possibly legally:

- Misrepresentation: do not represent yourself as something you are not in order to obtain information. This includes acquiring in-house telephone books, organizational charts, price lists and access to non-public organizational tours;

- Questioning job candidates: do not ask job candidates or new employees for confidential information about another organization;

- Consultants: be careful of what you ask of a consultant, especially regarding information about other clients.

Making contacts and visiting

Be friendly, open, and honest. Do not 'play games'. Be willing to listen, be polite, co-operative, and go for win–win. Do not misrepresent yourself or your purpose. Whatever information you ask for, you should be willing to reciprocate with the same information. Do not do to another organization anything you would not want done to yours!

An essential part of your benchmarking project will be visiting external organizations. There are various reasons for this. Unfortunately, sometimes visits are made for all the wrong reasons. For example, where a visit is made for the sole purpose of confirming that you are actually better, then it does not really get you any further down the chain of improvement. It simply has the effect of massaging a collective ego. You should also ensure that a visit to another organization is motivated by proactive rather than reactive reasons. Watch out for hidden agendas!

Before any visit is conducted, a thorough investigation of your internal business processes should have been made and at an early stage in your benchmarking initiative. A visit to an external organization will otherwise be fruitless as you will not know what you are looking for. You will not have sufficient information about your own processes to know what questions to ask. If you are not confident in this respect, it will not create the right impression on the host organization, nor lend itself to the formulation of a potential partner relationship.

If a focused approach to desk research has been taken, you should possess much secondary information not only in relation to best practice area(s), but in respect of potential best practice partners. Ask yourself whether you have enough relevant information regarding a particular organization to even make initial contact.

Try to draw up a list of best practice area(s) that you are interested in and match them with potential best-practice partner(s). There is some merit in telephoning them before sending any correspondence since it is an effective method of gauging how receptive they are going to be.

Before that initial telephone call is made with the chosen organization(s) you should ensure that you are not only able to answer most of the questions that they might ask, but that you are also able to give a focused and brief overview of your benchmarking initiative. For example, if during the conversation they ask for a copy of your process deployment flowchart, could you actually send it to them? Has it been completed?

You might like to consider some key areas before you contact a potential host organization. For example: who you are, your organization, what you are doing, why you want to visit, what you can offer them in return.

Subject to whether or not they are receptive, a follow-up letter can be sent confirming the details of the conversation and setting out in more detail your benchmarking initiative. This is an effective and professional means of opening up a channel of communication between yourself and the prospective benchmarking partner.

If undertaken correctly, a visit to another organization involves considerable preparatory work. It is essential to review the things which will have an impact upon the success of the visit before the relationship progresses any further.

At the beginning of the benchmarking initiative a team possessing appropriate skills should have been chosen. However, if the benchmarking initiative involves the whole department, does this mean to say that the whole department will be making the visit? Needless to say, it would not only be inappropriate for numerous people from your organization to take part in the visit, but could also become very complicated, time-consuming, and create an excessive burden for the host organization. A far more focused and structured approach can be made where just two or three key people with the right communication skills take part in the visit. This involves written, oral, and listening skills.

The chosen team then needs to decide what the roles of the team members will be. For example: who will be asking which questions? Who will be taking notes? This needs to be made clear and understood by each member so that messy, incoherent answers will not form part of the debrief.

The team should ensure that questions addressed to the host organization are clear, precise and centred around what they are looking to find. Simple, focused questions are more effective than rambling, complicated ones for achieving this purpose.

A questionnaire about the issues you want to address during the visit should be sent well in advance. Remember throughout your visit never to ask questions that your own organization would not be prepared to answer.

A pre-visit preparatory sheet should be completed by the team well in advance. This should include the responsibilities of each team member, together with a scheduled deadline before the visit for their completion.

There might be some merit in having a meeting before the visit or, at least, a conference telephone call. This should help to ensure that things run smoothly. At the meeting you should confirm dates and times of the visit; how information will be recorded and later used by your organization; whether a non-disclosure agreement is appropriate; contact points within both organizations; and the identity of people in the team. An agenda for the visit can then be agreed.

Agreements in relation to the above issues should be recorded and sent to the host organization. Once again, this will help to facilitate an efficient and effective visit.

During the visit, keep to the agenda and to the questions that were previously agreed. Many common sense pointers, such as how to behave during the visit can be gleaned from the benchmarking codes of conduct discussed in Chapter 10. Arrive at the agreed time, be courteous and introduce all members of the benchmarking team. Above all, try to keep to the agenda and to the agreed duration of your visit.

One common fault is using language that is not universal to all parties. Every organization, whether aware of it or not, subscribes to its own language or jargon; try not to slip into this during the visit. It will have the effect of excluding the host organization. Remember that you are there as a guest and should behave accordingly. Also, where visits to other organizations have previously been made, do not discuss that organization or the information collected unless you have prior permission to do so. Otherwise, you will not make a very good impression. Moreover, it shows a lack of professionalism and could constitute a breach of confidentiality.

After the visit, thank the host organization both in person and by letter. It is essential that where you have promised to share any outcomes that this is followed through. It shows you are reliable and will be a point in your favour should you wish to form a partner relationship.

An immediate debriefing of the benchmarking team is very desirable. Where it has been agreed, and where you feel comfortable enough, it might be possible to do this at the host organization. If, however, this has been planned for after the visit, then do it as soon as you can to maintain the accuracy of the information collected. This should then be disseminated to the rest of the benchmarking team.

Finally, do not be too disappointed if you have not collected all the information or got all the answers to your questions. Remember, this is only one visit, the purpose of which is to get a 'snapshot' of the host organization. Having said that, however, you should be in receipt of enough information to decide whether there is a possibility of forming a partner relationship.

Benchmarking partnerships

In the previous section we looked at visits to external organizations. It would be unusual to collect all the information required from a single visit, but you should have a good idea which organizations you are interested in, as well as the likelihood of their agreeing to such a partnership.

Considerable resources are invested in benchmarking projects. A slice of that investment will be taken up by the benchmarking partnership. So it is a good idea to make an analytical assessment of that partner before entering into the relationship.

A benchmarking partner relationship should be representative of something that encapsulates the true spirit of benchmarking – the mutual beneficial exchange of best business practice information which should lead to improved performance for all the organizations involved.

The resources required in time and money are significant. It follows then that a realistic expectation of organizations which decide to get involved in benchmarking partnerships is that they are going to get some beneficial results from such an investment. Some key questions to address from the very beginning, in respect of a potential benchmarking partner relationship are:

- What is in it for us and them?
- Why should we/they co-operate in this project?
- Do we have anything to offer them in return?

A benchmarking partnership opens up a channel of communication between organizations that would otherwise be closed. It is an ongoing dialogue. You should, therefore, also consider whether there is the right chemistry between the organizations. Some find it easier to develop a long-term benchmarking partnership with organizations that are similar to them in many aspects, such as in their organizational culture. It makes them feel more comfortable and so more confident in the partner relationship. More adventurous organizations look for organizations that are different from them in many respects.

BENCHMARKING IN THE PUBLIC SECTOR

The public sector is different

While TQM and benchmarking are as applicable to public admin-istration as to private sector manufacturing and service industry, their application in public administration is more problematical. There are many reasons for this, including:

- Staff culture and traditionally the lack of individual ownership, responsibility, client-care and staff empowerment;
- Historically bureaucratic and non-responsive systems;
- Lack of clarity about the multiple customers and stakeholders involved in even single transactions;
- Political, as opposed to market-determined, levels and extent of service, especially for subsidized and zero-priced services;
- Problems of scale and complexity associated with large, centralized organizations, sometimes with a large-scale technological basis.

The public administration sector, does, however, have a large potential for the development and improvement of its processes and procedures. This chapter explores the implementation of TQM and best practice benchmarking within the public sector.

TQM originates in public administration

In many senses public administration is the most natural place for the introduction of a total quality programme and benchmarking. Bureaucratic administrative structures are more likely to exist here rather than in the commercial world, where financial and competitive pressures mitigate against the growth of bureaucracy and assist us in recalling quite clearly the purposes for the existence of the unit and the importance of the customer. Historically in public administration such clarity of purpose has not always been apparent and the importance of the 'customer need' has not always been paramount.

In public administration it has often been the case that the provision of the service has not been that of a supplier to a customer, but rather that of an authority to a subject. Public administration may not be deliberately belligerent or malevolent but none the less the civil servants within the ministry concerned find themselves primarily as agents of the state carrying out an official state purpose, rather than service personnel involved in the provision of a defined service to a customer. Public administration was, after all, a monopoly; there was little concept of realistic pricing of service against market alternatives and the punitive power was in the hands of the public administrator rather than the customer; it was not that the customer could withdraw custom, but the public administrator could refuse to provide the service.

Against this background, the need for TQM was clearly greater than in the private sector. It is no surprise, therefore, that apparently the first usage of the phrase 'total quality management' was in the context of the American Department of Defense programme based upon the development of ideas of Deming and many others. The development of TQM has not neglected the areas of public administration or service. All over the world, government departments, agencies, public utilities and uniformed and non-uniformed public services have been amongst the forefront in TQM.

The application of TQM in
public administration

While the need is great and the origins early, the application of TQM and benchmarking in public administration is difficult. There are many reasons for this and one of the foremost is cultural. Increasingly, public administration is needing to move closer to the 'real world' in terms of financial accountability, management, quality assurance, and productivity and effectiveness. However, its history is one in which staff could be expected to have a job for life, to rise on time-served principles or perhaps connections; to have little incentive and much disincentive to show ingenuity, new thinking or effective teamwork; and, above all, not to question the system.

This backdrop is one to which the concepts of this book will seem particularly alien and this can make the process of getting TQM established difficult. Thus staff culture, the lack of individual owner-ship of the process of the public administration function, together with lack of any concept of client-care or staff-empowerment all represent negatives that need to be overcome by a TQM programme. Much of this has been changing over recent years, but not yet everywhere – old habits die hard!

The systems themselves tend to be bureaucratic and non-responsive. The lack of the incentive of the market place limits development of quick response, flexibility, simplicity and the availability of information on short timescales. So introducing these requirements for a TQM programme, is itself a big step. Bureaucracy and non-responsive systems are not just in themselves the opposite of what we are trying to achieve within TQM, they also hinder its introduction and slow its progress.

Even where there is the will to transform public administration, technical problems remain due to the limited nature of the TQM models in general use. A major orientation of most TQM models is the predominance of the *customer*. In public administration, this single-customer focus is not so clear; it is not just that there are multiple types of customers, but rather that there are multiple customers and stakeholders involved in even single transactions. For example, when a police officer arrests a potential criminal, is the officer's customer the criminal, the victim, witnesses, the courts, the Home Office or the community?

Public service organizations have attempted to solve this technical difficulty by introducing the *stakeholder* concept. Stakeholder models can now be found in many aspects of public service world-wide. For example, the Royal Mail identifies its stakeholders as customers, employees, shareholders and the community.

The problem, however, is that these generic stakeholder groups can tend to be somewhat unfocused in themselves. The community is, by its nature, a large and disparate group with divergent opinions on divergent issues. Lack of focus is what we are trying to avoid with TQM and benchmarking, and so much has to be done in the attempt to clarify. Even where this is done, at the operational level there is still a problem. Staff need clear priorities in their relations to the various stakeholder groups so that the organization can be focused towards their purpose for existing. This requires clear policy from the top, as well as staff discussion at all levels.

Another problem is that the market itself does not determine the level and extent of service. Decisions are taken at a political level and broadly there may be no limit to the demand for a zero-priced or subsidized service. This then creates shortfalls in the availability in service provision which appear to the customer as inefficiencies. The consequence is that confusion can remain in the customer's mind, the public, between productivity and quality. This problem is part of the nature of public administration and represents a particular challenge for staff.

Yet another problem is that public administration may necessitate large, centralized organizations, with associated complexity and problems of scale, combined with a bureaucratic management style. This implies that most employees will be a long way from the customer. Even front-line employees suffer, since they are a long way from decision making and are themselves at the mercy of internal systems. Such problems may be exacerbated if the organization has a large-scale technological base, such as in nationalized power provision, or a dependence upon a major computer system, such as perhaps in tax collection.

Strategies for success in the public sector

The potential problems of implementation of a TQM programme and benchmarking within public administration make it essential that specific strategies for success are sought. The following section examines some of those strategies, as well as looking at how the public sector as a whole has responded to this challenge. It also looks briefly at the situation in the USA, where TQM has been successfully implemented into federal departments.

TQM should become part of the 'real work' of a public sector department as early as possible. Senior management must realize that TQM cannot be delegated and that it is sensible for a steering group of the most senior managers to be set up at departmental or agency level. Ideally, this should be chaired by the most senior officer. For it is only in this way that TQM can become part of the overall job. The steering group will be able to identify and focus on the mission of the organization, the stakeholder groups, the intrinsic values and their purpose. The whole workforce should be involved in the quality improvement process, but it should commence top-down before returning bottom-up. While employee training will be necessary, two important aspects should be taken into consideration.

First, middle managers should be adequately prepared for the change in behaviours and, indeed, of attitude which will be expected and required of them for the programme to be successful. Second, cascade training is preferable to 'wall-to-wall' indoctrination. In cascade training, the members of the steering group themselves explain to their own staff: what the TQM programme is about; what they are intending to do in their own area; and perhaps come up with suggestions as to what staff may wish to do. At each level down the hierarchy, the same process is repeated; each manager explaining what it is all about and discussing how it may be implemented within their employees' area and what might be tackled first. With this system, each employee can put TQM in the context of their own job, which is typically not the reality with wall-to-wall training. It also dramatically reduces the amount of help that will be needed from outside consultants, although it is conventional for consultants to assist in the preparation of materials for cascade training and in the nature of the programme. Such assistance by experienced consultants is extremely important; and to this end the consultant may temporarily join the quality steering group.

A systematic approach to the quantification of quality and improvement is highly desirable, since otherwise the programme can be unfocused. This may be initially undertaken by a cost of quality approach or subsequently by the development of critical success factors. Both systems represent a unified approach to measurement, whether by looking at all the money that is wasted by doing things wrong and the prevention costs involved or, in the case of critical success factors, by identifying a small number of (preferably less than eight) critical success factors on which the progress of the organization will be judged. These measures then provide a yardstick for improvement activities lower down in the organization. Priority activities are those which impact on the measures most heavily.

TQM and benchmarking in US
public administration

Evidence of the growth of TQM in the public sector is illustrated by the situation in the USA where, in the 1980s, TQM became a prominent feature of public administration. Both NASA and the Department of Defense, during the Reagan and Bush administrations, made sustained efforts in relation to the implementation of TQM, as did other federal departments and agencies.

It was the Federal Quality Institute (FQI), which was largely instrumental in the promotion of TQM in public administration within the US government. The FQI, established in 1988, was part of the executive office of the president and acted as a primary source of leadership, information and consultancy service on quality management in the government. In 1995 the FQI was the subject of a downsizing programme and it is now the Office of Personnel Management (OPM) that is largely responsible for this function. This includes administering the quality awards for federal organizations. There are now three categories of awards; the Presidential Award for Quality, the Awards for Quality Improvement (replacing the Quality Improvement Prototype Award) and Quality Achievement Awards. The most prestigious award is the Presidential Award for Quality.

Between 1988 and 1997, there were six winners of the President's Award and 31 winners of what was known as the Quality Improvement Prototype Award. The 1997 winner of the President's Award was the US Army Infantry School and Center, Fort Benning, Georgia.

CASE STUDY: Inter-Agency Benchmarking and Best Practices Council

Another form of organization which is emerging and supporting bench-marking, best practices and leveraging knowledge in the US public sector is that of a 'virtual' organization. One such example is the Inter-Agency Benchmarking and Best Practices Council, which was created in August 1995 as a virtual, learning organization by six federal employees from five US public sector organizations. These were the Department of Energy, Department of Transportation, Department of Treasury, Internal Revenue Service, Patent and Trademark Office, and Department of Veterans Affairs.

In a true 'grass roots' effort, these six innovators worked independently and conceptualized and designed this organization. Working as a 'self-managed' work team, they discussed and established the council's priorities and created specific deliverables such as:

- An organizational charter;
- Declarations of commitment and support from their senior executives;
- Information brochures;
- Briefing materials;
- The first federal benchmarking and best practices conference;
- A home page on the World Wide Web.

The team embraced a philosophy and shared vision to help the US government be better prepared and more competitive for the future.

The council's objectives are to:

- Leverage capabilities, experience, and knowledge in benchmarking and best practices;
- Reduce duplication of efforts in the planning and conducting of benchmarking initiatives;
- Set a standard of excellence for benchmarking through the development of commonly agreed to definitions, ethics, and approaches;
- Create an environment which recognizes and rewards internal and external knowledge transfer.

The council uses several organizational structures to support its work. The council's charter members provide structure, the shared vision, and resources to support the projects. Senior executive service employees 'champion' the council and help secure resources. A third organizational structure manifests itself in the form of teams, each with a team leader, often a charter member. Each team assumes the role of process owner for a particular project. The fourth structure is the individual council members. At this time, only US federal employees with approval from their organizations qualify as council members. The credo of the council is that it is voluntary, self-organizing, and a 'working' council, which means that each member is to work actively on at least one project or initiative.

The council maintains partnerships with other organizations from the public, private, or non-profit sectors in support of specific projects. For example, the council's home page project includes the vice president's National Peformance Review, the treasury board secretariat, innovation and quality exchange of the government of Canada from the public sector; the American Productivity and Quality Center, the SPI Council on Benchmarking of the Strategic Planning Institute, the Benchmarking Exchange, the German Benchmarking Center (IZB), and business researchers' interests from the non-profit and private sectors.

Since its inception, the council has published a charter, obtained commitments from federal senior executive service employees to 'champion' the council, sponsored benchmarking training and member meetings, held the first ever national benchmarking and best practices conference for federal employees in November 1996, published a home page *(http://www.va.gov/ fedsbest/index.htm)* on the Internet, and includes a membership of some 170 federal employees who represent over 40 federal organizations.

Another significant project of the council is the Government Process Classification Scheme (GPCS). The council in partnership with the National Performance Review, developed this taxonomy so that organizations could capture, categorize, and transfer information about common processes across organizational boundaries. By using a scheme to codify functional or process knowledge, one can see an analogy to a 'Dewey decimal system' for applied knowledge database. The scheme also provides users a standardized best practices record for capturing best practice information through a simple data input record.

This GPCS was developed by a cross-section of federal government employes from both the executive and legislative branches. Team representatives from both the US General Accounting Office and the Library of Congress conducted exhaustive literature searches to obtain other viable taxonomies; however, most were limited to only private (profit) sector applications and lacked the comprehensiveness for cross-governmental use. By team consensus, the final framework was based on an agency enterprise model and expanded to include the wide range of general processes common to all US government agencies. Team members co-ordinated with external subject matter experts to include members of the MIT Center for Co-ordination Science, and the Brookings Institute.

For years, the US Office of Management and Budget in the executive office of the president, has been gauging labour and industry productivity using aggregates of task-level metrics (occupational classifications) and enterprise or 'establishment'-level metrics (Standardized Industrial Classification codes). The void between these levels is consumed by cross-functional process-level activities. With the new Government Performance and Results Act of 1993 (Public Law 103–62), US government agencies must better manage *process* information through strategic and performance planning and reporting. The GPCS will help agencies aggregate process-level data for analysis to discover benchmarks and best practices within their individual agencies and across government organizational boundaries.

As an example of applying the GPCS the US Air Force Center for Quality and Management Innovation is using the GPCS to classify best practices in their best practices clearinghouse concept. They have translated the GPCS into their own 'blue' language while maintaining the meaning of each process team number. The Air Force process classification scheme mirrors the numbering system of the parent GPCS, although several are changed to reflect the unique culture. By using the same numbering scheme, the council and the Air Force have a common basis for describing and sharing best practice information. The center also uses the GPCS standardized best practices record to capture and classify best practices.

Future plans of the council include publishing a benchmarking guide; establishing communities of practice on benchmarking and knowledge management; sponsoring another conference; and incorporating sophisticated conferencing capabilities into its home page.

Approaches of a similar nature are beginning to be seen throughout the world. A good example is the challenging and wide-ranging benchmarking projects being undertaken on an inter-state and local government level in Australia where benchmarking has been seen as a facilitator for improving the efficiency and effectiveness of government. This has provided some excellent data across some of their major activities which is being used both to highlight areas to be tackled, but also to help set demanding targets for improvement such as response times and unit costs.

Authors of Inter-Agency Benchmarking
and Best Practices:
Stuart Haggard, US Department of Veterans Affairs
Captain Donnie Williams, US Air Force
Jay Cavanagh, US Department of Energy

Quality of service and benchmarking in the UK public sector

In November 1991, a consortium was formed and sponsored by the development division of the Cabinet Office, which is now subsumed into the Office of Public Service. This consisted of 12 project leaders from 11 different departments and agencies. Their primary objective was to:

> encourage, co-ordinate and support projects ... which will enable departments and agencies to achieve demonstrable and continuous improvements in the quality of service they provide. Their aim was one of improving the quality of service offered by departments and agencies by taking into account best practice from both the public and private sector.

The 11 departments and agencies involved in the project were the:

- Benefits Agency (Central Derbyshire District);
- Central Office of Information;
- Civil Service College (London centre);
- Employment Service;
- Health and Safety Executive (research and laboratory services divisions);
- Home Office (Immigration Service);
- Inland Revenue (Capital Taxes Office and the Accounts Office, Cumbernauld);
- Lord Chancellors' Department (South-Eastern Circuit);
- Patent Office;
- Public Record Office;
- Department of Trade and Industry (North East).

The main focus of the programme was to develop standards relating to quality of service. This was achieved by establishing measures of quality of service which then enabled the setting of realistic standards derived from the priorities set down by customers. Research, therefore, had to be carried out to establish exactly what constituted the priorities of customers. Current performance could then be established, as well as targets for improvement of the service provided. Members of the consortium developed a two-fold approach; first they established measures which related to customers' understanding of the service and their degree of satisfaction with it, as well as establishing measures which related to the effective delivery of the service. From this they were able to use this information to set standards or benchmarks for future provision of the service.

The first stage was to gather initial data to help establish measurement and performance benchmarks which enabled members of the consortium to identify key issues to measure. Research methods were used for the establishment of satisfaction measures; the establishment of performance benchmarks and standards to review the effect and impact of changes in service methods (e.g., new services, different facilities); and to provide information to enable improvement and innovations to be implemented. Four areas were taken into consideration when measuring the quality of service; convenience of service; facilities and amenities available; provision of information; personal treatment.

Measurement against a set of standards is essential to the achievement of superior performance in any organization. There were three categories of measurement that the consortium took into consideration when setting targets to be achieved. These consisted of product, process and customer satisfaction.

Product measures were defined as those measures which focused on the fundamental issues which an organization believes are important to its customers. They are used to measure the satisfaction of the customer in relation to the processes of the service given to the customer. Satisfaction measures were defined as relating directly to the customer's interaction with the actual organization itself, while process measures were defined as relating to the running of the organization, those internal processes relating to the operational efficiency of the service.

From this information specific targets could then be set in different departments. For example, in relation to response times, the Patent

Office set a target of trying to reply in detail to correspondence within four to six weeks, as well as issuing examination reports within three months. At the Accounts Office (Cumbernauld) a target was set of processing all Giro credits by the day following receipt. And the Capital Taxes Office set a target for 80 per cent of correspondence to be dealt with within 28 days and 95 per cent within 56 days. In October 1995, the Deputy Prime Minister announced his intention to benchmark the performance of some of the government agencies against private sector companies and, eventually, other public services, both home and abroad. A pilot exercise run by the Cabinet Office involving 30 agencies was undertaken in 1996 using the business excellence model. This is to be followed up in 1997 with more agencies. A database of comparative data and best practices is being built up which should prove invaluable to those partaking in the exercise.

Some of the agencies have taken the initiative further. For instance, the Benefits Agency developed and introduced a quality framework which covered 12 specific elements. Each unit within the agency benchmarked itself against the framework. They were also encouraged to apply for a high-profile quality award which was presented to those who achieved a minimum score in each of the 12 elements and an overall demanding score. The award was important in its own right, but it was particularly so in identifying role models and good practices, enabling others to benchmark themselves against these exemplars. Many quite dramatic improvements were seen in a very short time particularly in the areas of improved accuracy levels, customer and community involvement, staff empowerment and efficiency savings. Indeed, one district office went on to make the shorlisted finalists in the UK Quality Award which included strong competition from private sector companies.

From April 1997 the Benefits Agency implemented a business excellence framework and award scheme which mirrors the European and UK quality awards and the business excellence model. This again will enable the units to benchmark themselves against the best in the public and private sectors.

It is interesting to note some of the standards which the consortium decided to benchmark performance against. The appearance of the Citizens' Charter has provided an added incentive for the improvement in the quality of service. The charter itself lays down distinctive aims in relation to the standards to measure performance against. The aims of the charter are to work for better quality in every public service, to give people more choice, to make sure that everyone is told what kind of service they can reasonably expect and to make sure that people know what to do if something goes wrong.

The charter standard established six key principles for the level of performance which can reasonably be expected from the public sector:

- Publication of the standards of service that the customer can reasonably expect and of performance against those standards;
- Evidence that the views of those who use the service have been taken into account in setting standards;
- Clear information about the range of services provided, in plain language;
- Courteous and efficient customer service, from staff who are normally prepared to identify themselves by name;
- Well-signposted avenues for complaint if the customer is not satisfied, with some means of independent review wherever possible;
- Independent evaluation of performance against standards and a clear commitment to providing value for money.

A scheme was established to recognize achievement against these standards with charter marks being awarded annually. In the case study above, all members of that project sought to apply the charter standards in their work with several of them applying for charter marks.

Other sources which provided a standard to benchmark against were the criteria of the Malcolm Baldrige National Quality Award (USA) and, increasingly, country and regional awards. These were found to provide valuable sources for quality improvement, as well as representing standards against which to benchmark.

Local government

Finally, at local government level, the UK has also seen the development of a benchmarking group; the Inter-Authorities Group. This has established a database of statistical benchmarking information. Local networks such as the Pembrokeshire benchmarking group have been established and the Audit Commission has formed a quality exchange to assist authorities in identifying best practices.

UK local government is not alone in its search for best practice. In Germany, the Bertelsmann Foundation established an international network and research activity for benchmarking local government to facilitate the establishment of future best practice. Members of the network consist of 10 local government bodies world-wide with best practice being developed through the international exchange of their local government experiences. The Quality Unit at the Nottingham Trent University contributed to the research funded by the Bertelsmann Foundation by examining the applicability of quality management issues to local government. Its paper together with other contributions made by members to the Bertelsmann Foundation can be found in *International Strategies and Techniques for Future Local Government* which is published by the Bertelsmann Foundation.

BENCHMARKING IN OTHER DIFFICULT AREAS: R&D, DESIGN AND THE CREATIVE SERVICE SECTOR

Dealing with creativity

In many senses creative people, or creative activities or departments are the most difficult when attempting to introduce quality improvement and total quality management (TQM). There is a natural aversion to quality assurance among the creative, since they believe it will stifle creativity and cannot be applied in an area which is 'not like making soap powder'. In many senses, this is as true among engineers and scientists in research and development (R&D) as it is among graphic designers, interior designers, journalists, chefs, textile designers and performing artists.

The apparent conflict between the free thought of creativity and the restrictions of structure associated with quality systems is not new and it remains one of the major challenges for the spread of implementation of ISO 9000 within the service sector. Such systems, however, do not have to be stifling of creativity and this justification or objection in any case masks other background concerns – fear of change and increased monitoring, lack of clarity of purpose, inability to find suitable measures of productivity and performance, and the like. With the correct level of senior management commitment and appropriate education, it is not fundamentally difficult to overcome these objections, although without this, these objections can be major delaying factors.

For TQM, rather than quality assurance, there is even less excuse that it stifles creativity, since the very purpose of TQM is to build the self-improving organization, putting to work the creativity of every individual within the organization, not just within their core jobs of work, but in order to improve the organization itself. Nevertheless, a common objection to TQM among creative professionals is that it is not appropriate to them and that, reading between the lines, it belongs in a manufacturing plant.

Clearly, progress is now being made in the introduction of total quality concepts into the broad spectrum of R&D, design and the creative service sector. The introduction of benchmarking into these areas as part of, or apart from, the introduction of TQM is particularly problematical. These areas are historically poorly systematized, so that defining business processes, finding benchmarking grids and finding meaningful comparisons, externally or even internally, are extremely difficult. Fortuitously, this problem is increasingly recognized and attention is increasingly being focused on how to approach it.

Following the introduction of Japanese approaches into management and production, R&D and product development is now under attack from Japanese simultaneous engineering practices. Justification for the introduction of these approaches, like those that have gone before in manufacturing and management, is based on a broad, crude benchmark of Western performance in these areas with that of Japanese companies. The whole area represents a benchmark of traditional Western development processes against Japanese ones in order primarily to accelerate time to market, cut development costs and failures.

Simultaneous engineering

The need for simultaneous engineering can be seen by looking at some of the things that are currently wrong in our design and development processes. The sorts of quotes that we often get that processes 'do not work', that the handover to manufacturing has 'taken place too early', that the area is 'not making soap powder' and that 'you cannot timetable creativity', illustrates the difficulty of applying quality tools and approaches to this area. Typically, in the design and development process we see backtracking and cycling, we see escalating costs, late delivery, poor quality and very often products which eventually are hard to make. There are also questions like: 'Does the customer really want what it is that we have designed?' And there are inter-departmental fences and suspicions, and fights and blame. There are barriers to information flow and we see our technical prima donnas, experts, and the isolation aspects and lack of teamwork.

Perhaps most notable of all, there is a lack of focusing tools such as quality function deployment, failure modes and effects analysis, and

Taguchi methods. There is also a lack of a comprehensive approach, a lack of discipline, a lack of clarity of purpose, and a lack of early involvement of suppliers and departments. The phrase often used to describe our current approach to development and design is 'over-the-fence engineering', whereby we eventually throw the product design over the fence, and manufacturing has to pick it up and do something with it. This, of course, causes panic and disruption, and indeed dubious quality.

Just as TQM has had its various pseudonyms, so does simultaneous engineering, often being described as parallel or concurrent engineering. In any case, the name is not so important. What we need to do, as with TQM, is to purpose-build for your company and, whether you call it simultaneous engineering in your design area, or quality improvement, it all comes to the same thing. The basic keys in TQM in the design and development process are the need for multi-disciplinary task forces, the need to define the product in customer terms and translate them into engineering terms, the need to optimize products and processes, and the need to design for manufacturing assembly. The special feature of simultaneous engineering is the simultaneous development of product, manufacturing equipment and processes, as well as quality control and marketing.

The methods of simultaneous engineering developed in Japan in the 1970s and 1980s, with names associated with the approach being those of Honda, Mazda, Nissan and Panasonic. In the USA it was not until the mid-1980s that we began to see the applications of simultaneous engineering in Chrysler, Ford, General Motors, Xerox and Digital. European applications have also been largely associated with the automotive industry such as Volkswagen, Daimler-Benz, Opel, Fiat and Krupp.

One feature of the approach of simultaneous engineering is the application of inter-functional task teams in much the same way that TQM uses these in other aspects of the business. In these teams we see representatives from product design engineering, manufacturing engineering, marketing, purchasing, finance, as well as suppliers and customers. Various team options are sometimes applied; the most successful approach perhaps being to have a simple pre-concept team of four or five individuals which is eventually expanded to a full task force at the concept stage. One reason for the success of simultaneous engineering in Japanese companies is that they tend to make their own special purpose machines or at least make them through subsidiaries. This is the pattern, for instance, in Honda, Nissan, Toyota and Mazda. This makes it easier to involve manufacturing engineers at an early stage.

A potential conflict between the approach of simultaneous engineering and the wider approach of TQM is the treatment of data. Simultaneous engineering tends to aim for data integration. One quote is that simultaneous engineering is 'wasted without Cad-Cam' and there is a desire to integrate data throughout the organization, right through from design to manufacture. In TQM we have tended to concentrate on the use of process data rather than historic data and, if we follow the approaches associated with Ishikawa, we tend to collect data as necessary and not set up large databases.

It is of interest to compare the bar charts for our conventional approach to engineering with those for simultaneous engineering as in Figure 9.1. In the conventional approach to engineering, we tend to start each stage of design and development later than in the simultaneous engineering approach. This gives us much greater time using simultaneous engineering to bring the product to the market in a safe and acceptable form.

Indeed, if we compare the Japanese and American automotive industries, we see that not only are there more engineering changes in the American automotive industry, but also, unfortunately, that these tend to take place at a later stage than in the Japanese industry (Figure 9.2). The consequence of this is that we are often problem solving after we have moved into the production phase. This, of course, is the worst time to solve problems, as early changes are much easier and cheaper to accomplish than subsequent ones. It also illustrates the point that Japanese companies can develop products much more quickly than their competitors.

Fig 9.1 Comparisons between conventional and simultaneous engineering

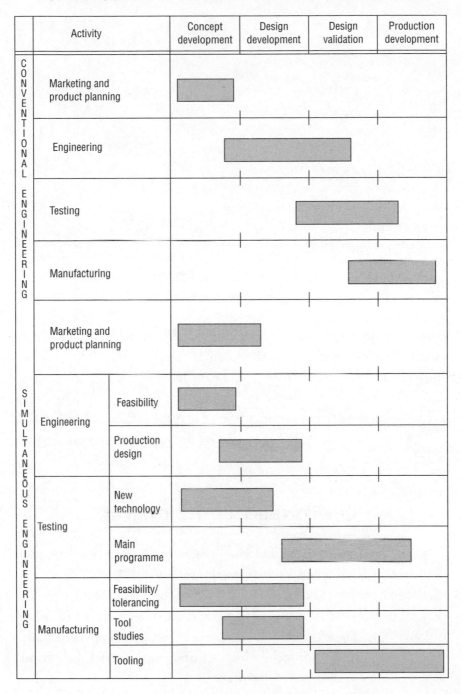

Fig 9.2 Problem prevention tackles issues well before production starts

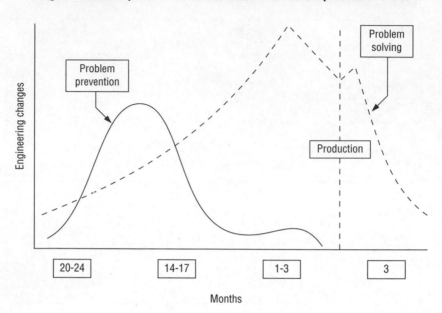

A consequence of late changes in the design and development process is that we tend to overshoot on timescales. This has a serious
implication in terms of costing. It means that we are in negative revenue for considerably longer and that, when we do eventually break
through into positive revenue, we have lost the potential for much of
the gain we may have made because we are not perhaps first into the
market.

Quality function deployment

The two major tools of simultaneous engineering are quality function
deployment (QFD) and Taguchi methodology. QFD is a team-based
methodology for incorporating the voice of the customer in the
design, development, manufacturing and marketing activities of the
organization. Taguchi methodology, in contrast, is an experimentally-
based prototyping approach, which can be employed at the various
stages in the development of product or service.

An interesting aspect of QFD is that it incorporates a benchmarking activity as part of the incorporation of the voice of the customer into product or service design, development, manufacturing and marketing.

QFD originated at Mitsubishi Heavy Industries in the early 1970s and was taken up by Toyota Autobody in the late 1970s. QFD is best thought of as an approach rather than a technique, since, like other Japanese methodologies it relies heavily on teamwork, and much of the benefit comes out of clear, concise team planning and communication.

QFD is a planning technique to ensure that the design of both products and processes are customer-focused. It uses a series of matrices – 'houses of quality' – to link customer needs with product or process features. On each matrix, customer needs are represented by rows, and product or process features or 'hows' are represented by columns. The body of the matrix gives the strength of relationships between needs and the way they will be, or are being, met. The roof of the house gives the correlation between the hows and the right-hand wing of the house gives a benchmark of performance in satisfying the needs against major competitors or possibly best practice. These aspects of the houses of quality tend to be fairly standard, but other aspects tend to vary between applications. A basic house of quality is illustrated in Figure 9.3. The bullseye symbol is used to represent a strong relationship, a circle a medium relationship and a triangle a weak relationship. Sometimes these are reserved for positive relationships only, with different symbols for the equivalent negative ones.

A further example is shown in Figure 9.4. This represents a house of quality for a retail laundry. From the house we see that a survey of customers has revealed that what matters to the customers are that the clothes are completely clean, that there is perfect press, that the correct clothes are returned and the correct service provided, and that there is a quick turnround and a friendly service. The customer survey also revealed that what was of most importance to the customer was not that the clothes were completely clean, but instead that the correct clothes were returned and the correct service was given. Accordingly, in the table this is represented by a weighting of five. The second most important aspect was viewed by the customer as a friendly service (four), then quick turnround (three), then perfect press (two), then completely clean (one).

Fig 9.3 Quality function deployment using a house of quality diagram

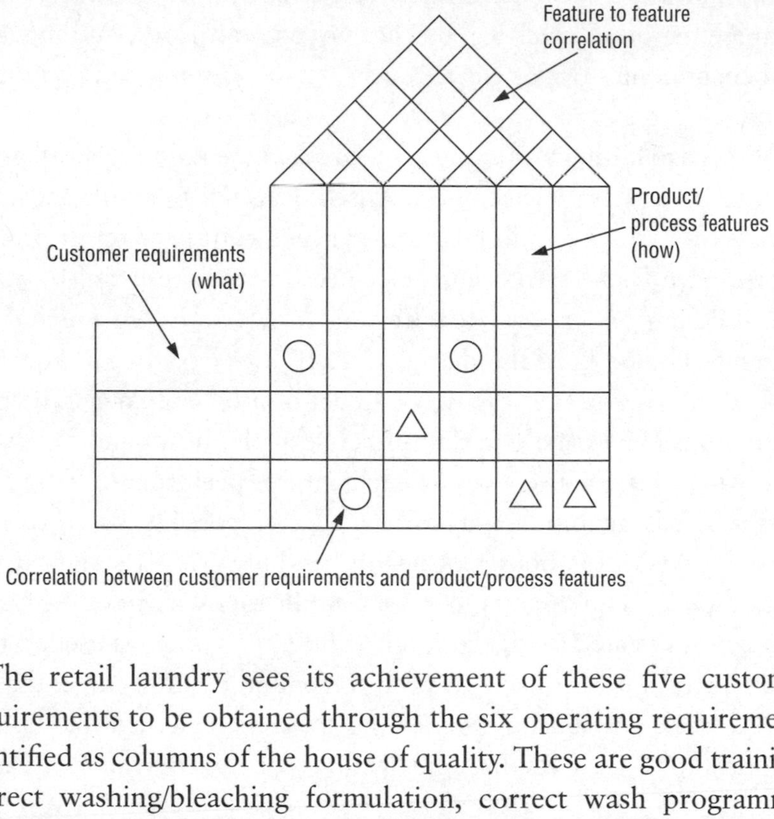

Feature to feature correlation

Product/ process features (how)

Customer requirements (what)

Correlation between customer requirements and product/process features

The retail laundry sees its achievement of these five customer requirements to be obtained through the six operating requirements identified as columns of the house of quality. These are good training, correct washing/bleaching formulation, correct wash programme, clean tumbler filters, correct moisture prior to colandering, and good equipment maintenance. Looking at the body of the table, we see that the most important aspect to the customer, correct clothes and correct service, only has a single (medium) relationship to one of the operating requirements, good training. This is also true for the second most important aspect to the customer, friendly service. The next most important aspect to the customer, a quick turnround, also has a weak dependence on good equipment maintenance. Interestingly enough, it is only the two least important customer requirements out of the five that we have identified, which are well supported by the operating requirements inside the organization; perfect press has a strong relationship with correct moisture prior to colandering and good equipment maintenance, as well as its medium relationship with good training. Completely clean clothes depends strongly on the correct washing/bleaching formulation, the correct wash programme, the cleanness of the tumbler filters and good equipment maintenance as well as having a medium relationship with good training.

In the roof of the house of quality we see the relationships between the various operating requirements that satisfy the customer requirements. Good training has medium relationships with the provision of the correct wash/bleach formulation, the provision of the correct wash programme, the provision of clean tumbler filters and the provision of correct moisture prior to colandering. Good equipment maintenance has medium relationships with clean tumbler filters and correct moisture prior to colandering. Other relationships, of course, may exist in reality.

The importance of the various operating requirements may be calculated from the importance of the customer requirements and the weightings given by the correlations in the body of the table. As an illustration, consider friendly service. This has a customer importance weighting of four and is connected to good training by a medium relationship which has a weighting of three. Friendly service, then, contributes four times three, which equals 12, to the importance weighting of good training. Proceeding in a similar way with each of the other four customer requirements, and in each case multiplying by three (because of the medium relationships with good training) and then adding up each of the contributions, we come to a total importance weighting of 45 for good training. For each of the other measures, proceeding similarly, we obtain the importance weightings shown in the table.

From these weightings it is clear that good training is the most important operating requirement, not because any customer requirement depends strongly on it, but because all customer requirements are related to it, albeit only by medium relationships. The next most important operating requirement is good equipment maintenance, followed some way back by correct moisture prior to colandering.

Fig 9.4 Quality Function Deployment in a retail laundry

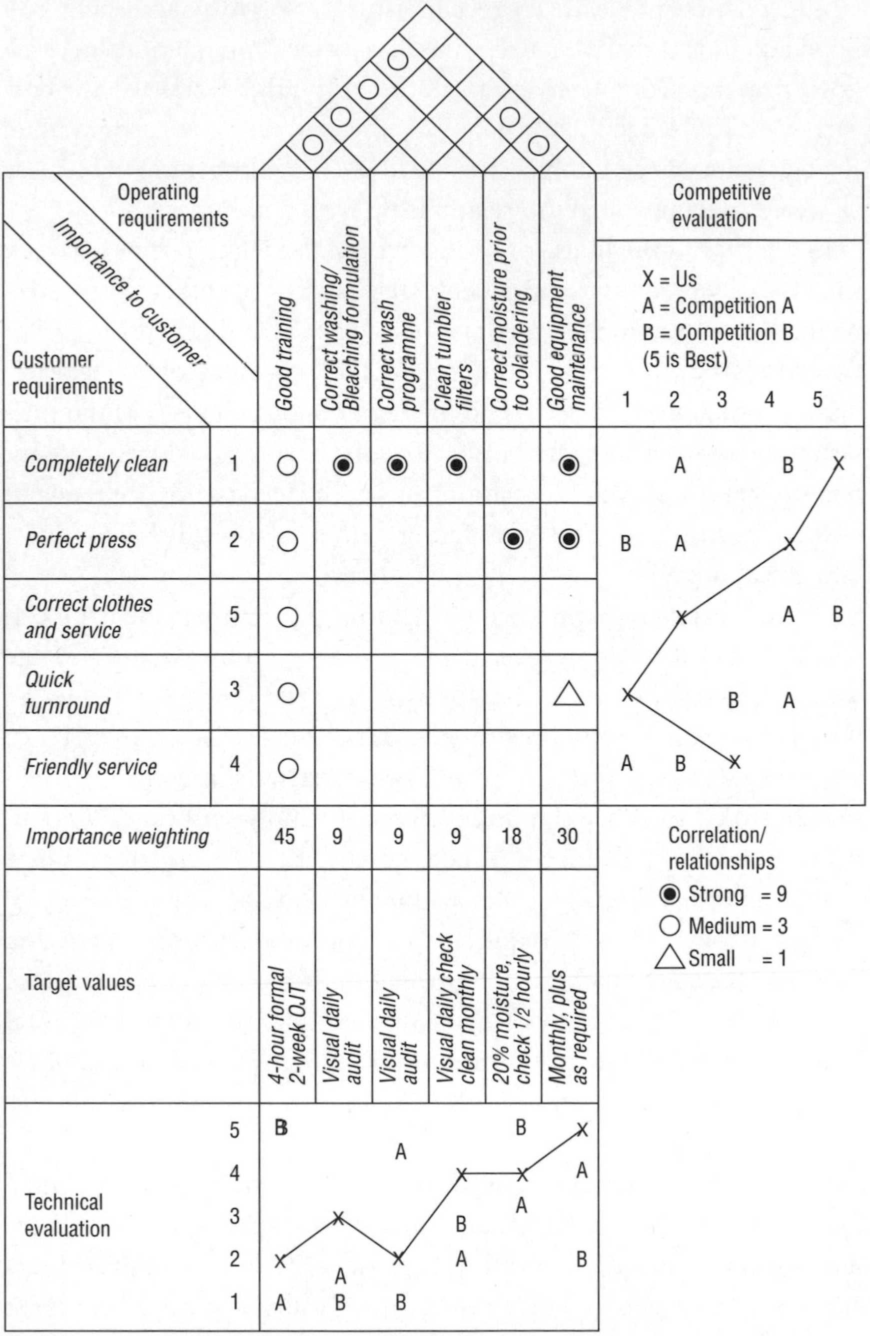

The three remaining operating requirements are of equal importance. These weightings will help to prioritize effort in terms of meeting the customer requirement. Clearly here, most effort must be given to ensuring and maintaining good training and good equipment maintenance.

If we now consider the right-hand wing of the house of quality, this contains information which benchmarks our performance as a retail laundry against that of our main competitors. For example, for completely clean clothes we can see that our customers have given us a rating of four, on a five-point scale on which five is the best, against a rating of three-and-a-half for our competitor B, and of two for our competitor A. We are clearly doing better. This is also true in terms of perfect press, where we are well ahead of both our competitors. We are also ahead on friendly service. However, we are behind on correct clothes and service, and quick turnround. This is particularly important for correct clothes and service, because this is regarded as most important by our customers. This benchmarking enables us to see that we must improve on correct clothes and service, and quick turnround to gain an edge over our competitors.

The basement of the house of quality contains the calculated importance weightings, and also target values and technical evaluations. The target values represent the targets on the operating requirements. The technical evaluation represents benchmarking our operating requirements against those of our competitors.

In product development applications of quality function deployment, a single house of quality would not be used, but several, as is illustrated in Figure 9.5. The first house (product planning) would translate customer wants into design requirements. These then form the input to the second house (part deployment) where design requirements are mapped to part characteristics. In the third house (process planning) part characteristics are mapped to key process operations, and in the fourth house (production planning) key process operations are mapped to production requirements. Other houses may be introduced as needed, for example for installation, if appropriate.

Fig 9.5 Product development application of quality function deployment

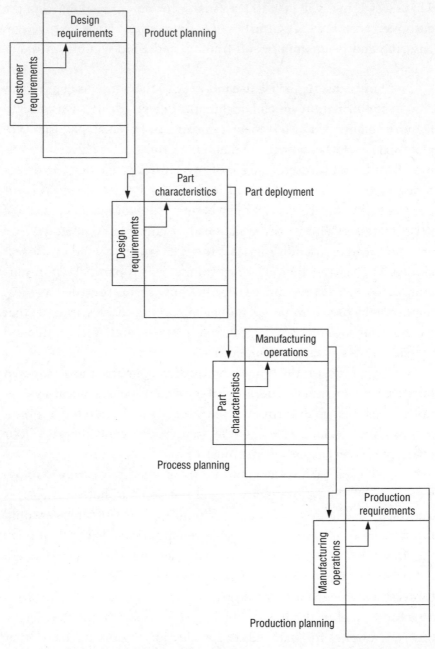

Applied correctly, quality function deployment should make use of an inter-functional team composed of representatives of all those involved in, or with interests in, the development of the product, or service, from market research through design, development, manufacturing and delivery to the customer. Small teams are preferable, of six to eight individuals of equal status. Specialists may be co-opted as needed. Open minds are needed, as well as experience.

Attendance at the series of team meetings should be a high priority. On major projects, perhaps as many as 60 hours or more of meetings may be required. These need to be in the project plan. Teams need training, and consensus, rather than voting, should be the order of operation among the personnel from production planning, research, design and development, marketing, product engineering, manufacturing, purchasing, service, installation, quality and tooling who may be involved.

First projects need careful implementation. Teams should be chosen carefully, as should be the project, and both should be monitored to ensure that things do not go wrong.

One possible set of steps for applying quality function deployment (in development) is shown in Figure 9.6. It is apparent that no high technology is needed, although specialist software has been marketed in this area. Little training in the technique is required, although training and mentoring is necessary to change the work pattern, to establish discipline and to help to remove the functional barriers. Also, little specialist skill is required since the complexity, which might at first sight be apparent in the method, really arises because we are no longer overlooking data which are overlooked in the conventional approach. There is also no knowledge loss, or repetition of work, with the QFD approach, and accordingly time and resource reductions claimed can be in the range from one-half to one-third. However, it must be stated that this is in companies which are mature in the use of QFD. First projects may add to normal development times. The use of QFD should include both basic and excitement features – in the case of the laundry, for instance, the basic cleaning process was not the most important aspect to the customer, who took this for granted. Similarly with an automobile, it is the aesthetic design features, not the basic functionality, which is often most attractive to a customer.

Fig 9.6 Steps in Quality Function Deployment

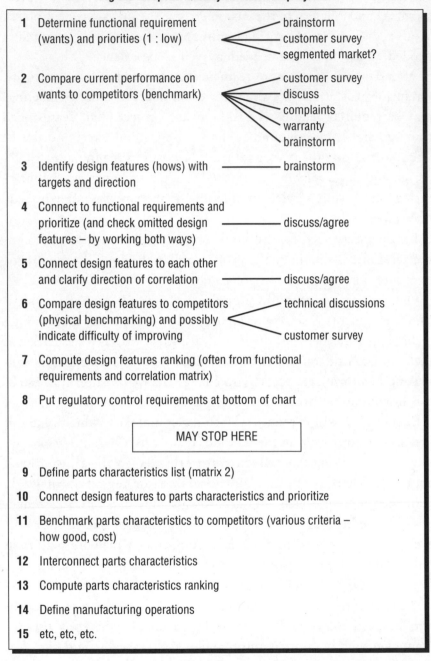

1   Determine functional requirement (wants) and priorities (1 : low) — brainstorm, customer survey, segmented market?

2   Compare current performance on wants to competitors (benchmark) — customer survey, discuss, complaints, warranty, brainstorm

3   Identify design features (hows) with targets and direction — brainstorm

4   Connect to functional requirements and prioritize (and check omitted design features – by working both ways) — discuss/agree

5   Connect design features to each other and clarify direction of correlation — discuss/agree

6   Compare design features to competitors (physical benchmarking) and possibly indicate difficulty of improving — technical discussions, customer survey

7   Compute design features ranking (often from functional requirements and correlation matrix)

8   Put regulatory control requirements at bottom of chart

MAY STOP HERE

9   Define parts characteristics list (matrix 2)

10   Connect design features to parts characteristics and prioritize

11   Benchmark parts characteristics to competitors (various criteria – how good, cost)

12   Interconnect parts characteristics

13   Compute parts characteristics ranking

14   Define manufacturing operations

15   etc, etc, etc.

Fig 9.7 Some benefits of Quality Function Deployment

- Improved quality
- Improved product reliability
- Reduced warranty claims
- Lower cost in design and manufacture
- Opportunity for improved profitability and improved company performance
- Reduced decision/planning time and improved decision making
- Improved productivity of technical and other staff
- A more customer-orientated workforce
- Better reaction to marketing opportunities

Used properly, QFD ensures discipline, structure and conformance to timescales which have been clearly stated. It also ensures a team attitude and breaches functional boundaries. It ensures recognition of customer satisfaction, and the anticipation and prioritization of customer needs. As a consequence of its use the customer only gets, and only pays for, what they require, and it helps in the development of a whole life-cycle attitude. QFD presents a continuous thread of information and communication throughout the organization. All aspects of quality of customer service are covered. It helps ensure attention to detail and detailed pre-planning. As a consequence of its use, actions and resources are also moved upstream, informed decisions are made and complex interactions clarified. By QFD we achieve problem avoidance which gives us competitive advantage. Some benefits of QFD are shown in Figure 9.7.

To achieve these advantages and benefits, however, QFD must:

- Be team-based, not committee-based;
- Have coherence;
- Have access to full market information;
- Be documented at each stage;
- Be reviewed and agreed at the next meeting;
- Be based on individuals bringing information into the meetings and doing work between meetings;

- Be disciplined;
- Focus on voice of customer;
- Have top-level commitment;
- Be open to the customer; and
- Be viewed as a process, not as a technique.

The difficulties that tend to arise in the applications of QFD are in themselves really advantages, since they force the clarification of issues which are often only implicit in the conventional approach. Thus, they force the resolution of these issues and the consistency of the development programme. Some such difficulties are shown in Figure 9.8.

Fig 9.8 Difficulties over advantages in clarification

1 Ignorant customers – especially on needs

2 Too late decisions or authorization to proceed

3 Lack of clarity in responsibility/authorization to define

4 Changes (iterations), e.g. in design features
   by others/management
   late
   in conflict with design philosophy or parts procurement policy, etc

5 Non-standard features/orders

6 Lack of attention to detail

7 First project and team

QFD has a good record in Japan, the USA and, increasingly, Europe. Companies such as Rank Xerox, Ford and Digital have achieved, in some cases, staggering results from the use of QFD techniques. However, automotive applications are still probably among the most common.

QFD techniques are often introduced as part of simultaneous engineering. In this approach, a multi-disciplinary task force is used as management, at a higher level, to ensure that there is simultaneous development of product, manufacturing equipment and processes, quality control and marketing. The product is defined in customer terms and translated into engineering terms by QFD.

Various versions of QFD and extensions to QFD have been developed. Numerous forms of houses of quality are in use within certain organizations, such as Motorola. A particularly interesting example of the extension of QFD, is that developed by Florida Power and Light (first international prize winners of the Deming Prize), known as the 'table of tables'. This is a matrix that cross-relates customer requirements and specific quality elements in internal administration, but which also pulls together all the different major customer groups within a single table.

Florida Power and Light sees a number of steps in the process of generating a table of tables. First, teams decide who the customers are; that is, they identify the major customer groups by de-aggregating the total market and services provided. The second step is to survey the customers to obtain data on needs. These are then weighted for importance and grouped into 19 quality elements. These elements include courteous customer service, continuity of service, environmental protection and so on.

The fourth stage is to begin to determine the relationship between the voice of the customer and company's internal activities. To do this, different customer groups are weighted, based on their size and usage of electricity. The fifth stage is to apply this weighting, ranked in importance with the 19 quality elements. In doing this, direct and indirect quality elements are combined; indirect elements correspond to those for organizations that represent and speak to the customer, such as a nuclear regulatory commission and the Florida Public Service Commission. Carrying on through this process, they arrive at the overall ranking of the quality elements.

The next step is to prioritize company activities based on what quality elements the customer identified as the most important. This stage being complete, it is then summarized on to one large sheet of paper – the table of tables.

This approach to the table of tables has been developed and fine-tuned over a number of years. However, it does not have to be complicated. Florida Power and Light uses the table to communicate the voice of the customer to all its employees. It is sent to every work location with instructions that it be set on the wall next to the bulletin boards, and in this way every employee can see what the customer thinks is important. Florida Power and Light has repeated this process annually.

Fig 9.9 Table of tables

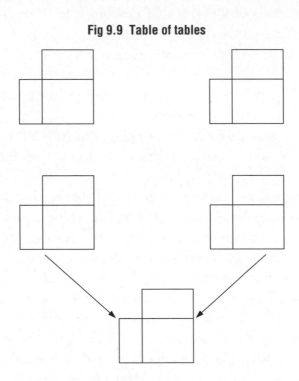

An illustration of the approach is shown in Figure 9.9. Individual houses of quality for the different customer groups are weighted and combined to form a single table of tables, while still retaining the visual impact of the individual customer groups and what matters to them. We can also see what matters to the aggregate and how the individual table of tables contribute.

This approach could, of course, be extended to other stakeholders, as well as just customer groups, so that a table of tables might combine the interests of various stakeholders. This, however, would be more complex and is currently the subject of development activity at Nottingham Trent University.

Introducing benchmarking into R&D

In the UK, interest in benchmarking within R&D is a key feature of the activities of a study group of the Quality Methods Association, and has been taken up by the Research and Development Society. However, a debate still exists as to whether benchmarking can be applied to the type of cognitive activity that R&D and design represent, rather to more basic process-based activities.

In practice, this is an academic debate, as simple brainstorming activity will reveal numerous potential applications, including simple first applications. The problem may, again, be one of attitude!

The creative service sector

Clearly, all management and service areas are candidates for quality improvement and benchmarking, and a very good way forward, as in other areas, is to define the fundamental business processes, identify the appropriate basis for measurement and to seek excellence to benchmark against. While the process is the same as elsewhere, the lack of definition and the problems of local attitudes can be major. Where organizations are already certificated, or seeking certification, to ISO 9000, much of this process of definition and clarity of business processes would have begun to have been put in place. Where it is not yet at that stage, the cultural shock can be quite severe, although it is not uncommon in the service sector to find aspects of competitor benchmarking well established in business practice. Two examples of this are in magazine publishing, where review of the creative content of competitors' magazines, as well as advertising sales, is common and in the practices of London hotels which regularly provide one another with information on nightly or weekly occupancy figures and room yields. Such analyses do concentrate perhaps more on outputs than on process measures, but nevertheless provide the basis for genuine benchmarking.

RELATIONSHIP TO INTERNATIONAL AWARDS CRITERIA

Introduction

Increased competitiveness, reduced cost and greater satisfaction among internal and external customers are but a few of the significant advantages from the implementation of a total quality management (TQM) programme within an organization. Realization of this, coupled with the need to survive within an ever-increasing competitive market place has inevitably led to a change in attitude by senior management towards the internal structure within an organization. It is not surprising, therefore, that many of the major business organizations have embarked on programmes to improve many of their management and business processes.

This increase in the awareness of the commercial advantages that the implementation of quality can bring to an organization has led to a positive increase in its recognition. This recognition has taken the form of the presentation of various prestigious awards as acknowledgements of achievements in the field of quality – indeed the criteria of the international awards are in essence benchmarks of quality representing marks of excellence to be achieved. Indeed, even if organizations do not wish to enter for the awards, the criteria of the awards may still be used in a practicable way as a guidance for internal improvement programmes.

Self-assessment and benchmarks

There is an increasing incentive for organizations to use the requirements of international awards as a means of evaluating their strengths and weaknesses for comparison with award winners and other organizations. Clearly, since winners of prestigious awards such as the Deming Prize and the UK Excellence Award are, by definition, world class companies, undertaking such self-assessment is a genuine benchmarking activity. (An example of an organization which uses the Malcolm Baldrige Award criteria for benchmarking its performance on a corporate basis is IBM.) Further, the awards provide effective benchmark grids which, like the case of ISO 9000 mentioned in Chapter 1, provide a structured basis for benchmarking. These awards, their background and their criteria are examined in this chapter.

The Deming prizes

The Deming prizes arose out of Dr Edwards Deming's lectures in Japan on quality control in the 1950s. The Union of Japanese Scientists and Engineers established the Deming prizes from royalties based on selling the lecture notes. There are two prizes, the Deming Prize, for individuals who have made significant contributions to the dissemination and development of theories relating to statistical quality control (SQC), and the Deming Application Prize, of which there are several different categories. This latter prize is awarded to companies which, in any financial year, have performed significantly well in the area of SQC. In 1989, Florida Power and Light (FPL) became the first non-Japanese organization to win a Deming prize.

In 1993, Eastman Chemical won the award in the manufacturing category. In 1994 AT&T Consumer Communications Services and GTE Directories Corporation won the service category, with Wainwright Industries Inc. winning the award in the small business category. In 1995 the two winners in the manufacturing category were Armstrong World Industries (Building Products Operation) and Corning Telecommunications. And in 1996, ADAC Laboratories and Dana Commerical Credit received awards in the manufacturing category with Custom Research and Trident Precision Manufacturing winners in the small business category.

It will be noted that there are not always winners in all categories.

Assessment criteria

Ishikawa's checklist (1980) for the Deming Application Prize criteria may be used by an organization to check both management and processes. A detailed list of criteria for the prize is shown in Table 10.1.

Table 10.1 Ishikawa's Checklist of Criteria for the Deming Application Prize

Category examined	Definition/explanation
1 Policy and objectives	Policy with regard to management, quality and quality control
	Methods in determining policy and objectives
	Appropriateness and consistency of the contents of objectives
	Use of statistical methods
	Dissemination and permeation of objectives
	Checking objectives and their implementations
	Relationships with long-range and short-range plans
2 Organization and its operation	A clear-cut line of responsibilities
	Appropriateness of delegation of power
	Co-operation between divisions
	Activities of committees
	Use of the staff
	Use of quality control circle
	(small group) activities
	Quality control audit
3 Education and its dissemination	Education plan and actual accomplishment
	Conspicuousness about quality and control, understanding of quality control
	Education concerning statistical concepts and methods and a degree of permeation
	Ability to understand the effects
	Education for sub-contractors and outside organizations
	Quality control circle (small group) activities
	Suggestion system
4 Assembling and disseminating information and its utilization	Assembling outside information
	Disseminating information between divisions
	Speed in disseminating information (use of computer)
	(Statistical) analysis of information and its utilization
5 Analysis	Selection of important problems and themes
	Appropriateness of the analytical method
	Use of statistical methods
	Tying in with own engineering technology
	Quality analysis, process analysis
	Use of results of analysis
	Positiveness of suggestions for improvement

Continued overleaf

Table 10.1 continued

Category examined	Definition/explanation
6 Standardization	System of standards Methods of establishing, revising and withdrawing standards Actual records in establishing, revising and withdrawing standards Contents of standards Use of statistical methods Accumulation of technology Use of standards
7 Control	Control systems for quality and related areas such as cost and quality Control points and control items Use of statistical methods such as the control chart and general acceptance of the statistical way of thinking Contributions of quality control circle (small group) activities Actual conditions of control activities Actual conditions of control system
8 Quality assurance	Procedures for new product development Quality development (breakdown of quality function) and its analysis, reliability and design review Safety and product liability prevention Process control and improvement Process capabilities Measurement and inspection Control of facilities/equipment, sub-contracting, purchasing, services, etc. Quality assurance system and its audit Use of statistical methods Evaluation and audit of quality Practical conditions of quality assurance
9 Effects	Measuring effects Visibility effects, such as quality, serviceability, date of delivery, cost, profit, safety, environment, etc. Invisible effects Compatibility between prediction of effects and actual records
10 Future plans	Understanding of the present conditions, and concreteness Policies adopted to solve shortcomings Plans of promotion for the future Relations with the company's long-range plans

The Malcolm Baldrige Award

In August 1987, President Reagan signed the Malcolm Baldrige Quality Act which established an annual US National Quality Award. This award is developed and administered by the Secretary of Commerce and the National Institute of Standards and Technology (NIST). The American Society for Quality Control (ASQC) assists in administering the award programme. It is primarily concerned with recognition of achievement in improving quality, the establishment by an organization of guidelines for self-evaluation and an expectancy that award winners will allow others to share in their experiences. This final factor is illustrated by participation of senior managers at the annual Quest for Excellence Conference which is usually held two to three months after presentation of the award.

Winners of the award in the manufacturing category have included such organizations as: Motorola Inc., Westinghouse Commercial Nuclear Fuel Division, Milliken and Company, Xerox Business Products and Systems, and the Cadillac Motor Car Company. In the small business category, winners have included: Globe Metallurgical Inc., Wallace Co. Inc., Marlow Industries; and in the service category, Federal Express Corp., AT&T Universal Card Services and the Ritz-Carlton Hotel Company.

More recently, in 1996 ADAC Laboratories, won the award in the manufacturing category, Dana Commercial Credit Corporation won the award in the service category, whilst Custom Research Inc. and Trident Precision Manufacturing won awards in the small business category.

Assessment criteria

Each year up to two awards may be given in each of three categories: manufacturing, service and small companies. The award criteria are centred around performance excellence with 'core values' being embodied in the following seven categories:

- Leadership;
- Strategic planning;

- Customer and market focus;
- Information and analysis;
- Human resource development and management;
- Process management;
- Business results.

The framework that connects each of the above categories is given in Figure 10.1.

Fig 10.1 Baldrige Award criteria framework

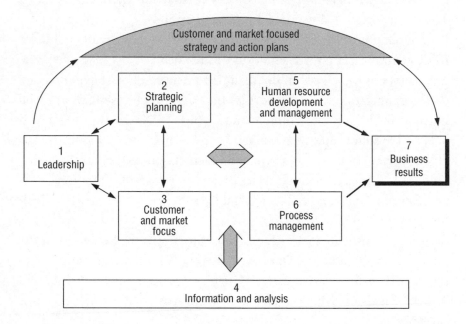

A point scoring system exists for each of the seven categories. The total points available is 1,000. An overview of the Baldrige Award criteria is given in Table 10.2.

Table 10.2 Criteria and scoring for the Malcolm Baldrige Award

Category	Areas to address	Points
1 Leadership Examines senior leaders' personal leadership and involvement in creating and sustaining values, company directions, performance expectations, customer focus, and a leadership system that promotes performance excellence. Also examined is how the values and expectations are integrated into the company's leadership system, including how the company continuously learns and improves, and addresses the societal responsibilities and community involvement	1.1 Leadership system 1.2 Company responsibility and citizenship	80 points 30 points
2 Strategic planning Examines how the company sets strategic directions and how it determines key action plans. Also examined is how the plans are translated into an effective performance management system	2.1 Strategy development process 2.2 Company strategy	40 points 40 points
3 Customer and market focus Examine how the company determines requirements and expectations of customers and markets. Also examined is how the company enhances relationships with customers and determines their satisfaction	3.1 Customer and market knowledge 3.2 Customer satisfaction and relationship enhancement	40 points 40 points
4 Information and analysis Examines the management and effectiveness of the use of data and information to support key company processes and the company's performance management system	4.1 Selection and use of information and data 4.2 Selection and use of comparative information and data 4.3 Analysis and review of company performance	25 points 15 points 40 points

Continued overleaf

Table 10.2 continued

Category	Areas to address	Points
5 Human resource development and management Examines how the workforce is enabled to develop and use its full potential, aligned with the company's objectives. Also examined are the company's efforts to build and maintain an environment conducive to performance excellence, full participation and personal and organizational growth	5.1 Work systems	40 points
	5.2 Employee education, training and development	30 points
	5.3 Employee well-being and satisfaction	30 points
6 Process management Examines the key aspects of process management, including customer-focused design, product and service delivery processes, support processes, and supplier and partnering process involving all work units. Also examined is how key processes are designed, effectively managed and improved to achieve better performance	6.1 Management of product and service processes	60 points
	6.2 Management of support processes	20 points
	6.3 Management of supplier and partnering processes	20 points
7 Business results Examines the company's performance and improvement in key business areas – customer satisfaction, financial and market place performance, human resource, supplier and partner performance, and operational performance. Also examined are performance levels, relative to competitors	7.1 Customer satisfaction results	130 points
	7.2 Financial and market results	130 points
	7.3 Human resource results	35 points
	7.4 Supplier and partner results	25 points
	7.5 Company specific results	130 points

European quality awards

In 1988, 14 of the leading Western European companies took the initiative of forming the European Foundation of Quality Management (EFQM). Their primary concern is to enhance the position of Western European organizations in the world market by stimulating and assisting the development of quality improvement activities, and by the acceleration of the acceptance of quality as a strategy for global competitive advantage. It is this organization, together with the support of the European Organization for Quality and the European Commission, which sponsors what is now known as the European Quality Award for Business Excellence. The award incorporates:

- European quality prizes awarded to a number of companies that demonstrate excellence in the management of quality as their fundamental process for continuous improvement;

- The European quality award itself which is awarded to the most successful exponent of total quality management in Western Europe.

The first award was presented in 1992 to Rank Xerox. In the same year quality prizes were awarded to BOC Special Gases, Industries del Ubierna SA, UBISA and Milliken European Division.

Former winners of the award have included Milliken European Division, Design Distribution Ltd, Texas Instruments (Europe) and Brisa, whilst former winners of the prize have included organizations such as ICL Manufacturing Division, Ericsson SS, TNT Express (UK) Ltd and BT.

The first step in an application for the award is the collation of a body of activity and results data from within an organization. This process is of significant value, for even if an organization is not successful in winning the award it will still be able to assess the level of commitment to total quality management and it will show the extent to which commitment to quality is being deployed throughout every level of the organization. Applicants must provide information about the following areas of the business:

- History;
- Organization chart;
- Technology and raw materials;
- Competitive environment;
- Partnership arrangements;

- Principal products and services;
- Customer and supplier base;
- Regulatory environment;
- Key product/service quality factors.

Assessment criteria

There are two essential aspects of the business excellence model, in Figure 10.2. These are *enablers* which concern the assessment criteria in relation to how results are being achieved and *results* which are concerned with the assessment criteria in relation to what the organization has achieved and is achieving. In accordance with the European model, processes are the means by which the organization harnesses and releases the talents of its people to produce results. Therefore, the processes and the people are the enablers which provide the results.

The model, Figure 10.2, was developed as a framework for the European award. It informs us that customer satisfaction, people (employee) satisfaction and impact on society are achieved through leadership driving:

- Policy and strategy;
- People management;
- Resources and processes.

These lead ultimately to excellence in business results.

The nine major categories of assessment criteria are shown in Figure 10.2 and detailed in Table 10.3 for the enablers.

Enablers

Table 10.3 gives an explanation of the various enablers as they contribute to the European model for self-appraisal and in Table 10.4 the criteria against which they will be scored are detailed.

Fig 10.2 European TQM model

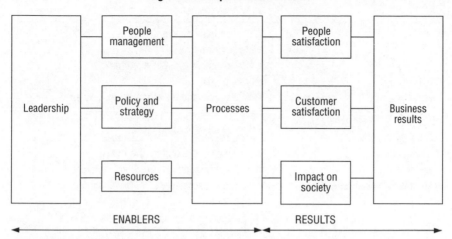

Table 10.3 European Quality Award for Business Excellence – criteria for enablers

Category	Areas to address	Points
1 Leadership How the behaviour and actions of the executive team and all other leaders inspire, support and promote a culture of business excellence as the best way to achieve the organization's objectives	1a How leaders visibly demonstrate their commitment to excellence and continuous improvement 1b How leaders support improvement and involvement by providing appropriate resources and assistance 1c How leaders are involved with their customers, suppliers and other external organizations 1d How leaders recognize and appreciate people's efforts and achievements	100 points
2 Policy strategy How the organization formulates, deploys, reviews and turns policy and strategy into plans and actions	2a How policy and strategy are based on information which is relevant and comprehensive 2b How policy and strategy are developed 2c How policy and strategy are communicated and implemented 2d How policy and strategy are regularly updated and improved	80 points
3 People management How the organization releases the full potential of its people	3a How people resources are planned and improved 3b How people capabilities are sustained and developed	90 points

Continued overleaf

Table 10.3 continued

Category	Areas to address	Points
	3c How people agree targets and continuously review performance 3d How people are involved, empowered and recognized 3e How people and the organization have an effective dialogue 3f How people are cared for	
4 Resources How the organization manages resources effectively and efficiently	4a How financial resources are managed 4b How information resources are managed 4c How supplier relationships and materials are managed 4d How buildings, equipment and other assets are managed 4e How technology is managed	90 points
5 Process The management of all value-adding activities within the organization	5a How processes key to the success of the organization are identified 5b How processes are systematically managed 5c How the processes are reviewed and targets set for improvement 5d How processes are improved using innovation and creativity 5e How processes are changed and the benefits evaluated	140 points

Table 10.4 Criteria for scoring enablers

1 The degree of excellence of your approach
2 The degree of deployment of your approach

Anecdotal or non-value adding	0%	Little effective usage
Some evidence of soundly-based approaches and prevention-based systems Subject to occasional review Some area of integration into normal operations	25%	Applied to about one-quarter of the potential when considering all relevant areas and activities

Table 10.4 continued

Evidence of soundly-based systematic approaches and prevention-based systems Subject to regular review with respect to business effectiveness Integration into normal operations and planning well-established	50%	Applied to about half the potential when considering all relevant areas and activities
Clear evidence of soundly-based systematic approaches and prevention-based systems Clear evidence of refinement and improved business effectiveness through review cycles Good integration into normal operations and planning well-established	75%	Applied to about three-quarters of the potential when considering all relevant areas and activities
Clear evidence of soundly-based systematic approaches and prevention-based systems Clear evidence or refinement and improved business effectiveness through review cycles Approach has become totally integrated into normal working patterns Could be used as a role model for other organizations	100%	Applied to full potential when considering all relevant areas and activities

Results

Just as enablers are scored, results can be similarly measured against the criteria given in Table 10.5.

Table 10.5 Results

Results	Score	Scope
Anecedotal	0%	Results address few relevant areas and activities
Some results show positive trends and/or satisfactory performance Some favourable comparisons with own targets	25%	Results address some relevant areas and activities

Continued overleaf

Table 10.5 continued

Results	Score	Scope
Many results show positive trends and/or sustained good performance over at least three years Favourable comparisons with own targets in many areas Some comparisons with external organizations Some results are caused by approach	50%	Results address many relevant areas and activities
Most results show strongly positive trends and/or sustained excellent performance over at least three years Favourable comparisons with own targets in most areas Favourable comparisons with external organizations in many areas Many results are caused by approach	75%	Results address most relevant areas and activities
Strongly positive trends and/or sustained excellent performance in all areas over at least five years Excellent comparisons with own targets and external organizations in most areas Best in class in many areas of activity Results are clearly caused by approach Positive indication that leading position will be maintained	100%	Results address all relevant areas and facets of the organization

Source: EFQM & British Quality Foundation, 1996

Results criteria are divided into four sections as detailed in Table 10.6. These are:

- Customer satisfaction;
- People satisfaction;
- Impact on society;
- Business results.

They are concerned with what the organization has achieved and is achieving. These can be expressed as discrete results, but ideally as a trend over a period of years.

The organization's results and trends for each result's criterion should be addressed in terms of:

- A company's actual performance;
- A company's own targets, and, wherever possible;
- The performance of competitors;
- The performance of 'best in class' organizations.

Self-appraisal should indicate the extent to which the organization's activities are covered by, and the relative importance of, the parameters chosen to measure results.

Table 10.6 European Quality Award assessment criteria for results

Category	Areas to address	Points
6 Customer satisfaction What the organization is achieving in relation to the satisfaction of its external customers	6a Customers' perception of the organization's products, services and customer relationships 6b Additional measures relating to the satisfaction of the organization's customers	200 points
7 People satisfaction What the organization is achieving in relation to the satisfaction of its people	7a The people's perception of the organization 7b Additional measures relating to people satisfaction	90 points
8 Impact on society What the organization is achieving in satisfying the needs and the expectations of the community at large	8a Society's perception of the organization 8b Additional indicators of the organization's impact on society	60 points
9 Business results What the organization is achieving in relation to its planned objectives and in satisfying the needs and expectations of everyone with an interest or other stake in the organization	9a Financial measures of the organization's performance 9b Additional measures of the organization's performance	150 points

UK quality awards

The British Quality Foundation was established to 'enhance the performance and competitive advantage of organizations in the UK, thereby ensuring their long-term success'. It administers the UK Quality Award for Business Excellence. Since the award was launched in 1994 by the then President of the Board of Trade, the award categories have been extended to include applicants from the public and voluntary services in 1996 and small businesses in 1997. (Specific guidance notes are available for organizations in the public and small business sectors.)

Assessment criteria

The assessment criteria are the same as for the European award (see Table 10.3 and Table 10.4) with special guidance notes being available for public and small business sectors.

Winners of the UK award

In 1994 there were joint winners, the Rover Group and TNT Express. In 1995, ICL High Performance Technology; and in 1996 again there were joint winners; Mortgage Express and Ulster Carpet Mills. To date there have not yet been any winners in the public, SME, or small business categories although there have been a number of public sector organizations on the final shortlist.

International awards criteria

Every year sees an increase in national awards based on or around the Deming, Baldrige or European/UK models. Most major European countries including Russia and Slovenia have awards, as well as Dubai. The common objective is to seek continuous improvement in order to be able to survive and compete in the long term.

The greatest benefit of all these self-assessment models, whether international, national, regional, state or city, is the opportunities that they provide for benchmarking. For example, award criteria can provide an internal benchmark for organizations and where an organization is large and consists of other companies in the group it can provide a means of measuring and comparing group performance. Ultimately, the criteria provide the opportunity to benchmark externally and on an international basis against other organizations.

Changes to the 1997 Business Excellence Model

In common with most of the award models, the European/UK system is reviewed regularly for improvement and appropriateness. There have been changes over the years with those for the 1997 version seeing an overall reduction in the sub-criterion parts from 33 to 32.

In criterion one, leadership, the word 'manager' is replaced by 'leader', which is more reflective of world class approaches. An additional criterion part has been introduced to people management of caring for people. In criterion four, the importance of supplier management has been recognized by the creation of a new part. The other changes in the results criteria are to simplify the model. Those changes in the results criteria are for ease of understanding and to encourage the linkage between 'enabler' and 'results'. Criterion six has greater emphasis on customer loyalty and in criterion seven more emphasis has been placed on staff motivation.

<u>LEGAL ASPECTS</u>

Introduction

Exchanging information to promote best business practice should not only be applied to the mutual satisfaction of all benchmarking partners, but also to the satisfaction of any third party that has the authority for imposing heavy penalties upon any actions that contravene the law. Whilst there appears to be a general acknowledgement that the law can affect benchmarking practices, there is little published information to help determine which practices are safe and which are not. The lack of case law does not make it any easier, however, nor should it be taken that this is indicative that benchmarking provides a field day for *all* organizations' activities in respect of exchanges of information.

Benchmarking codes of conduct

Helpful guidance on the way a benchmarking study should be conducted can be found in both the USA and the more recent European benchmarking codes of conduct. Both codes endorse a common sense approach to benchmarking. A good starting point therefore is to read through the codes. (Copies can be found at the end of this chapter.) Having said this, however, it should be remembered that the codes of conduct are guidance documents only. Indeed, the European code of conduct takes great care to stress that it does not represent a legal document and nor does adherence to it imply protection or immunity from the law.

How to cover yourself: three areas for attention

Having gleaned some pointers from the codes of conduct, the next stage is to address more specific areas and to understand how they could affect a benchmarking study. There are three appropriate areas of law:

- Confidentiality;
- Intellectual property law;
- Competition law.

We look at each of the above in turn, first, *confidentiality*. Much of the research undertaken during the information gathering stage will be based on already-published sources. Most secondary sources of information as indicated in Chapter 5 are in the public domain. However, primary sources of information, collected directly from the benchmarking partner might be subject to confidentiality. This means that where information has the necessary quality of confidence about it, then it will be subject to confidentiality. Benchmarking partners might therefore become subject to a confidentiality agreement either expressly or are implied from the nature of the relationship between the parties exchanging information.

A useful checklist for both parties might include:

- The constitution of confidential information i.e., what do the respective organizations stipulate as being confidential;
- Whether such information be distinguished from non-confidential information;
- Whether the necessary authority to exchange such information has been given;
- Whether any clause in employment contracts forbid such exchanges from taking place.

Before information is exchanged, the implications of employment contracts should be considered. For example, many contracts of employment, especially for individuals in a senior position, will contain express provisions in respect of confidentiality. However, even where there is no express condition there will still be an implied term in respect of this duty. With regard to exchanges of information made outside an organization, one of the issues that needs to be addressed is whether the implied or express provisions for confidentiality within contracts of employment restrict such exchanges. The dilution of con- fidentiality clauses in contracts of employment should not be an inadvertent outcome of any benchmarking initiative. Therefore, clarification is needed on exactly what can be exchanged with the benchmarking partner, together with the authority to exchange the information from the appropriate person.

Second, we consider *intellectual property*. A starting point in respect of a rather complicated area of the law is to try and define what exactly is meant by intellectual property. One rather extensive definition was put forward by the Works Intellectual Property Organization in Stockholm in 1967 which defined it as:

> The rights relating to; literary, artistic and scientific works; the performance of performing artists, phonograms & broadcasts; inventions in all fields of human endeavour; scientific discoveries; industrial designs; trade marks; service marks and commercial names and designations; and all other rights resulting from intellectual activity in the industrial, scientific, literary and artistic fields.

Whilst the legislation surrounding intellectual property rights has moved on considerably since 1967, this definition gives a good overview of some of the areas that it constitutes.

Intellectual property can be a valuable business asset and in some cases is *the* most valuable asset. Before exchanges of best practice information are made, organizations need to consider whether the information to be exchanged does include any intellectual property if so does it need to be protected before an exchange is made, should it be exchanged at all? It should be remembered that intellectual property can qualify for various forms of protection. For example, in the UK ideas and inventions can qualify for patent protection, designs can be protected by either copyright and/or under the Registered Designs Rights Act 1949 according to the type of design. Of course, confidentiality can cover all types of intellectual property, a prime example being the Coca-Cola recipe.

Finally, we consider *competition law*. The maintenance of healthy competition is necessary to sustain an economy and lends itself to improved research and design projects. A consequence of this can be improved, competitively-priced products and services, all to the good of the consumer. It can, however, be distorted. For example, where competitors network to make restrictive pricing agreements or where an organization with considerable market share abuses its position so as to prevent the emergence of new competition.

Competition law is an area where there appears to have been much concern expressed, particularly by larger organizations that have considerable market share or by benchmarking networks that exclusively attract organizations from single sectors. Where appropriate, organizations should consider the impact of the UK Restrictive Trade Practices Act 1976 together with Article 85 of the European Treaty of Rome, the provisions of the Sherman Act and the Federal Trade Commission Act. The penalties for infringing competition law can be exceptionally high. For example, where organizations are found to be infringing Article 85, a fine may be levied of between 1,000 to 100,000 ECU or up to 10 per cent of the turnover of the undertaking in the preceding business year.

Great care should therefore be taken in respect of benchmarking studies that involve direct competitors, especially where considerable market share is held by the benchmarking partners. The information that is being exchanged is of a confidential nature, ie it is not readily available in the public domain and such exchanges impact, or have the ability to impact, negatively on other organizations.

Non-disclosure and benchmarking agreements

Within any benchmarking study where exchanges of information are made, consideration should be given as to whether the activity would benefit from having a standard agreement in place. The most obvious reason for this is accuracy. An agreement can help to facilitate the accurate recording of what is being exchanged by whom and when. The existence of such an agreement might also help to assure any third party that there has been no infringement. Some suggestions that organizations may wish to include within such an agreement have been incorporated within the Pitman/Financial Times *Benchmarking Workout* book, and organizations may wish to consider the following:

• The underlying principles governing conduct throughout the duration of the agreement;

- Financial considerations;
- The presence and role of a third party facilitator;
- Annual review;
- Identification of material to be exchanged;
- The purpose(s) for which the exchanged material is to be used;
- The purpose(s) other than for which the material is to be used;
- Liability in relation to employees and subsidiary organizations;
- A provision for the return of the material/information;
- Termination of the agreement;
- Remedies for breach.

THE BENCHMARKING CODE OF CONDUCT

Preamble

Benchmarking – the process of identifying and learning from best practices anywhere in the world – is a powerful tool in the quest for continuous improvement and breakthroughs.

To guide benchmarking encounters, to advance the professionalism and effectiveness of benchmarking, and to help protect its members from harm, the International Benchmarking Clearinghouse, a service of the American Productivity & Quality Center, has adopted this code of conduct. Adherence to this code will contribute to efficient, effective and ethical benchmarking.

CODE OF CONDUCT

1.0 Principle of Legality

1.1 If there is any potential question on the legality of an activity, consult with your corporate counsel.

1.2 Avoid discussions or actions that could lead to or imply an interest in restraint of trade, market and/or customer allocation schemes, price fixing, dealing arrangements, bid rigging, or bribery. Don't discuss costs with competitors if costs are an element of pricing.

1.3 Refrain from the acquisition of trade secrets from another by any means that could be interpreted as improper including the breach or inducement of a breach of any duty to maintain secrecy. Do not disclose or use any trade secret that may have been obtained through improper means or that was disclosed by another in violation of duty to maintain its secrecy or limit its use.

1.4 Do not, as a consultant or client, extend benchmarking study findings to another company without first ensuring that the data is appropriately blinded and anonymous so that the participants' identities are protected.

2.0 Principle of Exchange

2.1 Be willing to provide the same type and level of information that you request from your benchmarking partner to your benchmarking partner.

2.2 Communicate fully and early in the relationship to clarify expectations, avoid misunderstanding, and establish mutual interest in the benchmarking exchange.

2.3 Be honest and complete.

3.0 Principle of Confidentiality

3.1 Treat benchmarking interchange as confidential to the individuals and companies involved. Information must not be communicated outside the partnering organizations without the prior consent of the benchmarking partner who shared the information.

3.2 A company's participation in a study is confidential and should not be communicated externally without its prior permission.

4.0 Principle of Use

4.1 Use information obtained through benchmarking only for purposes stated to the benchmarking partner.

4.2 The use or communication of a benchmarking partner's name with the data obtained or practices observed requires the prior permission of that partner.

4.3 Contact lists or other contact information provided by the International Benchmarking Clearinghouse in any form may not be used for purposes other than benchmarking and networking.

5.0 Principle of Contact

5.1 Respect the corporate culture of partner companies and work within mutually agreed procedures.

5.2 Use benchmarking contacts, designated by the partner company if that is the partner's preferred procedure.

5.3 Obtain mutual agreement with the designated benchmarking contact on any hand-off of communication or responsibility to other parties.

5.4 Obtain an individual's permission before providing his or her name in response to a contact request.

5.5 Avoid communicating a contact's name in an open forum without the contact's prior permission.

6.0 Principle of Preparation

6.1 Demonstrate commitment to the efficiency and effectiveness of benchmarking by being prepared prior to making an initial benchmarking contact.

6.2 Make the most of your benchmarking partner's time by being fully prepared for each exchange.

6.3 Help your benchmarking partners prepare by providing them with a questionnaire and agenda prior to benchmarking visits.

7.0 Principle of Completion

7.1 Follow through with each commitment made to your benchmarking partner in a timely manner.

7.2 Complete each benchmarking study to the satisfaction of all benchmarking partners as mutually agreed.

8.0 Principle of Understanding and Action

8.1 Understanding how your benchmarking partner would like to be treated.

8.2 Treat your benchmarking partner in the way that your benchmarking partner would want to be treated.

8.3 Understand how your benchmarking partner would like to have the information he or she provides handled and used, and handle and use it in that manner.

BENCHMARKING PROTOCOL

Benchmarkers:

- Know and abide by the Benchmarking Code of Conduct.

- Have basic knowledge of benchmarking and follow a benchmarking process.

- Prior to initiating contact with potential benchmarking partners, have determined what to benchmark, identified key performance variables to study, recognized superior performing companies, and completed a rigorous self-assessment.

- Have a questionnaire and interview guide developed, and share these in advance if requested.

- Possess the authority to share and be willing to share information with benchmarking partners.

- Work through a specified host and mutually agreed upon scheduling and meeting arrangements.

When the benchmarking process proceeds to a face-to-face site visit the following behaviours are encouraged:

- Provide meeting agenda in advance.

- Be professional, honest, courteous, and prompt.

- Introduce all attendees and explain why they are present.

- Adhere to the agenda.

- Use language that is universal, no one's own jargon.

- Be sure that neither party is sharing proprietary information unless prior approval has been obtained by both parties, from the proper authority.

- Share information about your own process, and, if asked, consider sharing study results.

- Offer to facilitate a future reciprocal visit.

- Conclude meetings and visits on schedule.

- Thank your benchmarking partner(s) for sharing their process.

BENCHMARKING WITH COMPETITORS

The following guidelines apply to both partners in a benchmarking encounter with competitors or potential competitors:

- In benchmarking with competitors, establish specific ground rules up front, e.g., 'We don't want to talk about things that will give either of us a competitive advantage, but rather we want to see where we both can mutually improve or gain benefit'.

- Benchmarkers should check with legal counsel if any information-gathered procedure is in doubt, e.g., before contacting a direct competitor. If uncomfortable, do not proceed, or sign a security/non-disclosure agreement. Negotiate a specific non-disclosure agreement that will satisfy the attorneys from both companies.

- Do not ask competitors for sensitive data or cause the benchmarking partner to feel that he/she must provide data to keep the process going.

- Use an ethical third party to assemble and 'blind' competitive data, with inputs from legal counsel in direct competitor sharing. (Note: When cost is closely linked to price, sharing cost data can be considered to be the same as price sharing.)

- Any information obtained from a benchmarking partner should be treated as internal, privileged communications. If 'confidential' or proprietary material is to be exchanged, then a specific agreement should be executed to indicate the content of the material that needs to be protected, the duration of the period of protection, the conditions for permitting access to the material, and the specific handling requirements that are necessary for that material.

Source: 'Surveying Industry's Benchmarking Practices', International Benchmarking Clearinghouse (1992) Houston, Texas.

THE EUROPEAN BENCHMARKING CODE OF CONDUCT

This code of conduct is the result of a consultation and development process co-ordinated by the Performance Improvement Group with the help of the Eurocode Working Group. This group comprises senior benchmarking managers and legal representatives from the following organizations:

BT, DTI, EFQM, IFS International, KDPMG Peat Marwick (USA), Shell International, Siemens, the Benchmark Network, the Post Office, the Quality Unit at the Nottingham Trent University.

Contributions were also gratefully received from the following:

APQC, BQF, Prudential Assurance, SIQ, SPI, the Benchmarking Centre UK, the Benchmarking Club Italy, the Law Society, the Quality Network.

Introduction

Benchmarking – the process of identifying and learning from best practices in other organizations – is a powerful tool in the quest for continuous improvement and performance breakthroughs. The authors and sponsors have produced this European code of conduct to guide benchmarking encounters and to advance the professionalism and effectiveness of benchmarking in Europe. It is closely based on the widely used APQC/SPI Code of Conduct promoted by the International Benchmarking Clearinghouse, and the authors gratefully acknowledge this source. The working has been modified to take into account the rules of European Union competition law. The layout and presentation have been modified to take into account the rules of European Union competition law. The layout and presentation have been modified to proved a more positive chronological approach.

Adherence to this code will contribute to provide, effective and ethical benchmarking.

1.0 Principle of Preparation

1.1 Demonstrate commitment to the efficiency and effectiveness of benchmarking by being prepared prior to making an initial benchmarking contact.

1.2 Make the most of your benchmarking partners' time by being fully prepared for each exchange.

1.3 Help your benchmarking partners prepare by providing them with a questionnaire and agenda prior to benchmarking visits.

1.4 Before any benchmarking contact, especially the sending of questionnaires, take legal advice.

2.0 Principle of Contact

2.1 Respect the corporate culture of partner organizations and work within mutually agreed procedures.

2.2 Use benchmarking contacts designated by the partner organization if that is its preferred procedure.

2.3 Agree with the designated benchmarking contact how communication or responsibility is to be delegated in the course of the benchmarking exercise. Check mutual understanding.

2.4 Obtain an individual's permission before providing their name in response to a contact request.

2.5 Avoid communicating a contact's name in open forum without the contact's prior permission.

3.0 Principle of Exchange

3.1 Be willing to provide the same type and level of information that you request from your benchmarking partner, provided that the principle of legality is observed.

3.2 Communicate fully and early in the relationship to clarify expectations, avoid misunderstanding, and establish mutual interest in the benchmarking exchange.

3.3 Be honest and complete.

4.0 Principle of Confidentiality

4.1 Treat benchmarking findings as confidential to the individuals and organizations involved. Such information must not be communicated to third parties without the prior consent of the benchmarking partner who shared the information. When seeking prior consent, make sure that you specify clearly what information is to be shared, and with whom.

4.2 An organization's participation in a study is confidential and should not be communicated externally without their prior permission.

5.0 Principle of Use

5.1 Use information obtained through benchmarking only for purposes stated to and agreed with the benchmarking partner.

5.2 The use or communication of a benchmarking partner's name with the data obtained or the practices observed requires the prior permission of that partner.

5.3 Contact lists or other contact information provided by benchmarking networks in any form may not be used for purposes other than benchmarking.

6.0 Principle of Legality

6.1 If there is any potential question on the legality of an activity, you should take legal advice.

6.2 Avoid discussions or actions that could lead to or imply an interest in restraint of trade, market and/or customer allocation schemes, price fixing, bid rigging, bribery, or any other anti-competitive practices. Don't discuss your pricing policy with competitors.

6.3 Refrain from the acquisition of information by any means that could be interpreted as improper including the breach, or inducement of a breach, of any duty to maintain confidentiality.

6.4 Do not disclose or use any confidential information that may have been obtained through improper means, or that was disclosed by another in violation of a duty of confidentiality.

6.5 Do not, as a consultant, client or otherwise pass on benchmarking findings to another organization without first getting the permission of your benchmarking partner and without first ensuring that the data is appropriately 'blinded' and anonymous so that the participants' identities are protected.

7.0 Principle of Completion

7.1 Follow through each commitment made to your benchmarking partner in a timely manner.

7.2 Endeavour to complete each benchmarking study to the satisfaction of all benchmarking partners as mutually agreed.

Principle of Understanding and Agreement

8.1 Understand how your benchmarking partner would like to be treated, and treat your partner in that way.

8.2 Agree how your partner expects you to use the information provided, and do not use it in any way that would break that agreement.

Important Notice:

This code of conduct is not a legal document. Though all due care has been taken in its preparation, the authors and sponsors will not be held responsible for any legal or other action resulting directly or indirectly from adherence to this code of conduct. It is for guidance only and does not imply protection or immunity from the law.

BENCHMARKING PROTOCOL

Benchmarkers:

- Know and abide by the European Benchmarking Code of Conduct.
- Have basic knowledge of benchmarking and follow a benchmarking process
- Should have:
  - Determined what to benchmark,
  - Identified key performance variables to study,
  - Recognized superior performing organizations,
  - Completed a rigorous internal analysis of the process to be benchmarked, before initiating contact with potential benchmarking partners.
- Prepare a questionnaire and interview guide, and share these in advance if requested.
- Possess the authority to share and are willing to share information with benchmarking partners.
- Work through a specified contact and mutually agreed arrangements.

When the benchmarking process proceeds to a face-to-face site visit, the following behaviours are encouraged:

- Provide meeting agenda in advance.
- Be professional, honest, courteous and prompt.
- Introduce all attendees and explain why they are present.
- Adhere to the agenda.
- Use language that is universal, not one's own jargon.
- Be sure that neither party is sharing proprietary or confidential information unless prior approval has been obtained by both parties, from the proper authority.
- Share information about your own process, and, if asked, consider sharing study results.
- Offer to facilitate a future reciprocal visit.
- Conclude meetings and visits on schedule.
- Thank your benchmarking partner(s) for sharing process.

BENCHMARKING WITH COMPETITORS

The following guidelines apply to both partners in a benchmarking encounter with competitors or potential competitors:

- In benchmarking with competitors, ensure compliance with competition law.

- Always take legal advice before benchmarking with competitors. (Note: When cost is closely linked to price, sharing cost data can be considered to be the same as price sharing.)

- Do not ask competitors for sensitive data or cause the benchmarking partner to feel he/she must provide such data to keep the process going.

- Do not ask competitors for data outside the agreed scope of the study.

- Consider using an experienced and reputable third party to assemble and 'blind' competitive data.

- Any information obtained from a benchmarking partner should be treated as you would treat any internal, confidential communication. If 'confidential' or 'proprietary' material is to be exchanged, then a specific agreement should be executed to indicate the content of the material that needs to be protected, the duration of the period of protection, the conditions for permitting access to the material, and the specific handling requirements that are necessary for that material.

Source: British Quality Foundation (BQF).

DO'S AND DON'TS

Introduction

This chapter considers some of the do's and don'ts of successful benchmarking. It does not attempt to suggest that there is an A-Z for successful benchmarking. Note that the points are neither given in order of importance nor in order of conduct. However, it does examine some of the fundamental issues to be considered by organizations, before, during and after embarking upon a benchmarking initiative.

Does a performance gap exist in your organization?

A genuine loss of profit within an organization is no joke, but in an ever-increasing competitive market place it is, for many organizations, becoming all too commonplace. This identification of loss of profits is merely the first step, leading to the following questions.

- Why has this happened?
- What is the difference between a successful competitor's performance and our own?
- Who are the best performers in relation to what we do?
- What do we do about improving our own performance?

All need to be considered. Identification of a performance gap is then merely the first step. Improvement of performance and how an organization sets about increasing its share in the commercial world is the next.

Commitment from the top

One of the most desirable factors for stimulating and encouraging a benchmarking initiative is top executive commitment and responsibility. It is therefore essential that commitment from the top may be relied upon once a decision has been taken to embark upon a new business strategy. This sort of commitment may be engendered from the beginning in terms of training and education as to what benchmarking is, how it can be used for the good of the organization and how to implement those changes within the organization.

The need for change within an organization is usually identified by senior management. However, once a performance gap has been identified and a positive approach to implementing new initiatives taken, it will not be effective unless the whole workforce sees a positive commitment from the top ranks. Management should be active members of the benchmarking team; this ensures their responsibility for the project. A benchmarking initiative must be planned and, as with other major programmes of change, there must be a company policy in relation to it. This ensures continuity and clarity for those people in the benchmarking team, as well as those outside.

Activity must be steered and reviewed if the organization is to receive benefits from the initiative. The only way this may be accomplished is if management take responsibility. It follows that the right things are done at the right time in the best interests of the company. Top management must therefore be responsible for continuity, commitment, policy objectives and the direction which the benchmarking initiative will take. If positive improvements are to take place within an organization, benchmarking must be taken seriously by all involved.

As with any new organizational strategy there must be an underlying belief in the need for the change. If there is a positive belief in the need for change from within an organization, then something worthwhile will eventually be accomplished. It is essential therefore for management to generate continuous enthusiasm for changes within the organization and for the initiatives bringing those changes.

The importance of top management commitment was illustrated by a survey from the American Productivity Center. According to this, top management commitment was the most important factor for driving a benchmarking initiative throughout an organization. Lack of support from management can have a negative effect on benchmarking and is, according to the survey, seen as a contributory factor to unsuccessful benchmarking projects.

The benchmarking team

Benchmarking is a team effort and a team approach should be taken. However, it is always practical to have one or maybe two people who will act as facilitator(s) for the team. Of course, the involvement of a facilitator will depend upon the individual personalities of the team. Some organizations prefer to have a full-time facilitator while others use the teamwork process as a means of self-facilitation.

The individual team members should consist of those people who are directly responsible for the processes which are to be benchmarked, the process owners, with perhaps also representatives from within those departments which the benchmarking exercises directly effect.

Flavour of the month syndrome

All too often organizations will suffer from the 'flavour of the month' syndrome, where organizations look for quick solutions to long-term problems. Benchmarking is not a quick fix to long-term problems and should not been seen as such; otherwise you will be disappointed. Initial results from benchmarking may not be easily identifiable. Therefore if you choose to benchmark, do not expect a quick fix in relation to problems.

Benchmarking as part of strategy

To be really effective, benchmarking should become part of the regular management agenda; more than that, it should become part of organizational strategy. Benchmarking is a natural progression of total quality management (TQM). The two should be connected, for they are complementary. The aim is to establish a benchmarking initiative as an on-going process with full integration into the organizational structure. Establishment of best practice within an organization, after a while, becomes the natural way of doing things.

Internal business processes

Before embarking on any new initiative, it is essential that you become familiar with your own internal business processes. In fact, knowledge of an organization's internal business processes has been cited as being one of the most important factors for benchmarking. Almost all of the organizations which took part in a US survey saw this factor as being of 'great' or 'very great' importance to a successful study. A major part of this is understanding the critical success factors in your company, i.e., those factors upon which the success or the failure of the organization can be measured. If you do not know what they are, then it naturally follows that you will not know which processes to benchmark.

Full familiarization with an organization's internal processes may take anything between two months and a year depending on the size of the organization. One of the pitfalls is not following this process through thoroughly. This can result in the benchmarking team arranging an external visit to collect information before they are actually ready to make the best use of the visit. These visits result in frustration and irrelevant data – a needless, wasteful and disappointing journey.

Processes to benchmark

Familiarization with important internal processes is the key to understanding which are to be benchmarked. Any activity within an organization that can be measured can be benchmarked, which means that both functional and generic processes may be tackled.

Functional benchmarking involves a comparison with those organizations which are not direct competitors – but which do carry out similar functional activities. The advantages of functional benchmarking are many: it is easy to identify similar functional areas in many organizations and confidentiality is not usually an issue, making the exchange of data between organizations considerably easier. Generic benchmarking may be defined as the benchmarking of those business processes which cut across various functions but in quite different industries. The advantage of this is that the various approaches are likely to be diverse, creating the most innovative breakthroughs for improvement. However, it follows that the processes to be benchmarked will be those which the organization depends upon to survive in the commercial environment.

While any activity can be measured and benchmarked, most companies will start with those areas where they know they need to be competitive to remain in business. The company should have a clear mission statement or list of business goals which is used to focus improvement activity. Customer satisfaction is high on most company priority lists, as is the need for a low-cost operation. Deciding these broad areas partly answers the question: Where do we want to be? These broad areas, however, need to be broken down into more specific activities that can be measured. What are the processes that deliver customer satisfaction? Which processes eat up the costs? The more precisely you define what you need to measure, the more useful will be the information that you gather to compare it with. What things are important to customers? What will help them to be successful? How good is the service currently given? And so on.

Benchmarking research

Benchmarking must be based on planned research, inclusive of both internal and external sources. As a direct consequence of the benchmarking boom, information has become more accessible. The starting point is material from within your own organization. Perhaps another part of the organization has carried out benchmarking before – find out before researching external sources. Internal information is always useful; it is relevant to what your organization does.

Information from external customers is also useful. What do they think is the most important process in your organization? Contacts within the same business are also useful; if they have carried out successful benchmarking initiatives they might be willing to share information. Consultants, academics and industrial observers are all relevant sources of information. All of these sources should be supplemented by data obtained from business literature, that is periodicals, TQM magazines, trade journals and material available in libraries, and from benchmarking conferences/workshops, seminars, annual reports, public databases, research institutions and government agencies.

Choice of partner or target

A good way of choosing a partner or target is to start by listing those processes which are considered to be essential to the survival of the organization and then asking the question 'Who, or what, is better than us?'

When looking for an appropriate partner do not dismiss internal choices. Where an organization is large and there are different sites in different regions then internal comparisons can be successfully made which may result in improved performance. It is very easy to make internal comparisons between departments, sites or even companies within the same group. The advantage here is that exchange of information may not be covered by strict confidentiality agreements and that no direct competition is involved, making information inaccessible. In addition to this, the organizations may share the same politics, ethics, culture, language, etc all of which make the process more simple. Visits are straightforward to arrange and information is readily available. Operations are often similar across sites and so benchmarking these activities is considerably easier than processes in an external organization.

A choice of an internal partner may effectively cut across many barriers, however, the real improvements within an organization come from comparisons with external partners. External partners may either be found in other businesses which are part of the same group or they may be selected regardless of business, industry sector or location as best practice partners.

Remember that a choice of an external partner is far more difficult. Benchmarking visits to competitors will, by their very nature, be problematical. However, the best way to work with a competitor may be by both organizations signing an agreement as to what material will be exchanged in relation to success and best practice. This will, hopefully, avoid misunderstandings between the organizations and open up a channel of communication for the future. Of course, databases, company reports, etc are always a useful way of looking at another organization's activities and performance.

Visiting the partner

Once a partner has been chosen, decide before the visit exactly what it is you are trying to achieve from the visit. The benchmarking team must be fully conversant with the purpose of the visit, as should the partner you have chosen to benchmark. Questionnaires should already have been sent to the proposed partner, in addition to communicating your expectations from the session with the partner. Perhaps one of the best ways of accomplishing this is to send them an agenda setting out what you expect to cover during the time you are at their organization.

It is also important to establish a relationship with the organization you have chosen to be the benchmarking partner; once the channels of communication have been well and truly opened the process of exchanging information naturally becomes easier. Before your visit it should be agreed upon by both organizations exactly what material is to be exchanged, never asking for material from the partner that you would not also be willing to furnish them with.

Most benchmarking activity will be governed by some form of mutual non-disclosure agreement. This means that the material you obtain from the partner must normally not be used for purposes other than those originally agreed. If you do wish to use the material, perhaps to give to a third party, do not use it without prior consent.

A structured professional approach to another organization is imperative; it will help you get the best information from that organization. If there is a mutual benefit for both parties, even better; it encourages organizations to be more open and more willing to exchange data.

Use the checklist in Figure 12.1 or one of your own to optimize your visit.

Fig 12.1 Optimizing your visit to the partner to be benchmarked

1 Ensure that sufficient desk research has been carried out, using both internal and external sources

2 Check that adequate questionnaires have been sent to the benchmarking partner, and that these have been completed and thoroughly analyzed

3 Find out whether exchange of information is to be based upon written guidelines. This will usually take the form of confidentiality/mutual non-disclosure agreements

4 If there is no set procedure in relation to the third point above, try and establish an agreement with the partner to be benchmarked, which does not compromise either party

5 Before your visit, discuss with the partner the content of the information to be exchanged, in order to avoid any misunderstandings

After the visit, treat all contacts made through the benchmarking activity as confidential. Obtain prior permission before reference is made either to the material obtained from the benchmarking partner or to a third party when in an open forum. In addition to all of this, take into consideration the legal aspects of benchmarking. You can use benchmarking codes of conduct, as put forward by the International Benchmarking Clearinghouse in the USA, as a guide.

Record your study

Throughout the benchmarking initiative, material will be researched, collated and stored. This should be put onto a database. Not only is this good practice, it also acts as a safety net by ensuring that the benchmarking material is easily accessible, by the benchmarking team, and others who may want to carry out a benchmarking exercise of their own. The same ground will not be covered twice if there is a permanent record of all benchmarking research.

The level for benchmarking

Organizations which do have a significant market share by their very nature will have different requirements in relation to benchmarking than the smaller organization which might just be wanting to improve its quality initiative. It therefore follows that the larger organizations will, out of necessity, search for those organizations who are 'best in the class', to maintain their place in the commercial market. In contrast, some smaller organizations can also benefit from the good practices of the larger, successful organizations in general.

Analysis and use of data

Once all information has been collected, data should relate both to the current performance of the organization and to those practices used by the benchmarked partner. The next stage is to compare the organization's current performance with the partner. The conclusion that an organization may reach is that its own performance is actually superior in some of the areas benchmarked, but there will still be lessons to be learnt. If you reach the conclusion that your performance is inferior, then there will be more major lessons. The organization will be able to focus itself upon a set of criteria or quantified goals based upon the knowlege about its own performance and the performance of the organization with which it benchmarked.

Implementation

Once the decision is made to proceed, implementation of the changes must be planned and steered. New targets for the critical activity can be set based on the benchmark data and good leadership will be essen-

Table 12.1 Troubleshooting

Problem	Likely causes	Solution
Benchmarking the wrong measure	Inadequate knowledge of own organization and operations	Further research to find significant measure
Benchmarking the wrong organization	Inadequate desk research	More detailed initial research
Benchmarking not leading to action	Senior management not involved	Ensure that management is seen to be in support
Failure to sell idea to senior management	Lack of information, poor presentation	Tie best practice benchmarking firmly to the existing business plan; show how other companies have benefited
Lack of resources for benchmarking	Lack of management support; exclusive ownership by the best practical benchmarking team	Lobby and promote best practice benchmarking as a company-wide approach
Data not meaningful	Too much/too little data; data not comparable	Tighter focus to measures; test the assumption about your processes that generated the measures
Inaccurate/false data	Over-reliance on public or competitor sources	Double-check sources through personal checks
Failure to sell data to target organizations	Scepticism and protective instincts	Make clear the benefits of shared information; re-assess criteria for selection of partners
Over-reliance on superficial similarity with partner	Lack of rigorous criteria for assessing partners	Redefine search find closer fits
Benchmark partner unwilling to share useful data	Benchmark partner too alike	Define search by process not industry
Benchmark too many measures	Unclear priorities	Relate best practice benchmarking to business plan

Source: 'Best Practice Benchmarking', DTI, 1992.

tial to maintain focus and prevent backsliding. Progress towards the new objectives will need to be reviewed regularly, and senior management has a key role in overseeing and providing support for the implementation process.

The on-going initiative

The most successful organizations are aware that improvement is a never-ending journey. Benchmarking is part of this journey and can be seen as a tool to change practices within an organization. As such, it is a continual process and should be regularly reviewed – ensure that it is put on a regular agenda.

Troubleshooting

Throughout your benchmarking various problems may arise. Use Table 12.1 as a guide for troubleshooting problems.

EXAMPLES OF BENCHMARKING APPROACHES AND EXPERIENCES

Introduction

Learning from the first-hand experience of others is what benchmarking is all about. The aim of this chapter is to give readers an overview of approaches and experiences based on organizations that have undertaken benchmarking. Brief case studies reflecting a range of approaches and levels of maturity follow. Some of those presented have been written by people who actually undertook the benchmarking study.

Benchmarking at Bell Canada: improving customer satisfaction

Bell Canada, the largest Canadian telecommunications company, provides both long-distance and local service to more than seven million customers in Ontario and Quebec. In June 1992 the Canadian long-distance market opened up to competition. This spurred Bell Canada's customer focus effort through benchmarking.

Deregulation affected the industry more than anyone anticipated. Bell Canada saw a rapid and huge loss in market share, a consequence of which was the commencement of a three-year transition plan to move from a monopoly organization of 110 years to a market-driven organization focusing on what the customer really needed. It was believed that a significant improvement would be harnessed through the use of benchmarking.

Historically, customer satisfaction surveys undertaken at Bell Canada indicated that customer satisfaction was high. However, this was contradicted by the equally high level of complaints received by its answer centre. Based on this conflicting information, Bell Canada decided to use benchmarking as a tool to determine what other world-class organizations did to achieve high customer satisfaction results. In June 1993, a benchmarking team was formed to study how the company could significantly improve customer satisfaction. The team included answer centre employees (regional managers, front-line manager, client representatives who represent customers), the union, the corporate measurement group, and two facilitators from

Bell Canada's internal benchmarking group. To get the team focused on the project, one of the first steps was to identify team roles and create a project plan. The time scale over which the study was to be completed was six months. Importantly, there was top management support for the study.

Determining customers' expectations

Early on in the study, the benchmarking team decided to look behind the customer survey results. They set out to find which key service attributes customers valued the most and then built a survey around customer satisfaction. More than 200 customers were telephoned to determine what was most important to them and how the answer centres rated in those specific areas. A result of this was the identification of three important areas:

- Access – accessibility at a time and by a method convenient to customers;
- Resolution of service issues – how flexible Bell Canada is, how knowledgeable, and how willing the organization is to take time to listen and resolve a problem;
- Treatment – how friendly and caring Bell Canada is in meeting customers' needs.

Table 13.1 illustrates the performance ratings for each of these categories, as viewed by customers. These ratings provided the baseline data that allowed Bell Canada to compare itself with other organizations. The customer data confirmed to the team that benchmarking was an appropriate improvement tool to identify breakthrough enablers to facilitate significant change.

Table 13.1 Customer ratings of Bell Canada

Percent of customers rating 'very good' or 'excellent'

(5 or 6 on a scale of 1–6)	
Access	47.3%
Resolution	70.9%
Treatment	68.6%
Overall Satisfaction	**78.5%**

Approach to the study

A rigorous methodological approach was taken by the team. Before the team went on to identify potential study partners, they had to further define key operational issues that related to fulfilling customers' needs. They also realized the importance of looking at organizations based outside the telephone industry. Through secondary research using a variety of sources including customer input, the benchmarking team invited 20 organizations to participate in a high-level metric screening survey. The survey, which involved a 45-minute phone call, discussed overall customer satisfaction, customer satisfaction measures and technology.

Fifteen organizations completed the screening survey, two of which were within Bell Canada. The team then discussed the criteria with the company names being made anonymous. This allowed them to focus on 'true' best practices and not allow company bias to creep in. Eight organizations survived this process and were invited to participate as best practice partners. Only five of these organizations moved on to the second phase. These were MCI, Chemical Bank, Land's End, IBM Canada and Polaroid Corporation.

The second phase included a four-hour telephone interview to gather more data. This enabled the team to get into the *hows* and *whys* of customer satisfaction. This exercise led to the preliminary identification of best practices in the operational areas that had been identified. The team then went on to select three of the five best practice partners for site visits. These partners represented the highest utilization rate of the 21 best practices identified. In addition they were strong performers in areas where Bell Canada was weak. Table 13.2 compares Bell Canada with three best practice companies.

Table 13.2 Utilization rates of best practices in partner companies as determined from primary research

Best practice usage rates	
Company A	92.1%
Company B	78.9%
Company C	81.6%
Bell Canada	**19.0%**

Before the site visits could take place, members of the benchmarking team developed questionnaires in small groups specific to each of the five organizations, with the questions being tailored to reflect six to seven best practices for each organization.

Analyzing the data

Following the two weeks after the site visits took place, the benchmarking team analyzed the information. The common metric that was used to normalize performance results was net satisfaction index. This allowed different rating scales to be compared on equal terms. From the site visit information, Bell Canada drafted 21 best practices that were linked to the three customer criteria. These were *access*, *resolution* and *treatment*. Seventeen of the 21 best practices were prioritized for immediate implementation. These included all of those that supported resolution and treatment customer criteria.

A unique aspect of the benchmarking study was that the team created a customers come first implementation team and a leadership team to implement the findings from the study. The 17 best practices were implemented within Bell Canada during an 18–36 month period, from January 1994 to December 1996. Goals were then created to direct the implementation effort in the following four categories:

- Culture;
- Market driven;
- Learning organization;
- Excellence.

The 17 best practices were then streamlined according to one of the appropriate four categories.

Focusing on the customer

The implementation team established five teams to address five specific best practices:

- Communication;
- Education;
- Customer care;
- Process improvement;
- Coaches.

The first team established communication channels to ensure a free, two-way flow of information. This helps client representatives to have access to current information and resources to fully satisfy customers regarding pricing, strategy, products and services. The education team is responsible for developing training for all new employees. A seven-week course trains employees on the workstation, customer service, and selling skills, as well as giving employees the opportunity to perform role playing and spending 18 days working with real customers on the phone. The customer care team handles complex issues and executive complaints for three answer centres. Their goal is to establish customer loyalty. External customers can access the team directly or be transferred from a business unit.

As a result of the benchmarking study, significant changes were seen throughout the entire organization. This affected both customers and employees. Table 13.3 illustrates how Bell Canada has improved since May 1993. It represents three site visit results compared with Bell Canada's target and pilot site results, whilst Table 13.4 illustrates some of the major changes to the customer and culture as a result of the implementation plan.

Table 13.3 Customer results from the new answer centre

Customers rating 'very good' or excellent' for new answer centre				
	May 93	*Best observed*	*Target*	*Pilot site (March 1996)*	*Bell Ontario (March 1996)*
Access	47.3%	95.0%	80.6%	75.0%	64.0%
Resolution	70.9%	90.0%	93.0%	88.0%	79.0%
Treatment	68.6%	95.0%	93.1%	92.0%	86.0%

Table 13.4 Impact of implementation plan

CUSTOMER

Before:	*Transformation to:*
Unclear values	Guiding principles
Focus on regulator	Focus on customer satisfiers
Inconsistent standards	Customer-based contact standards
Internal needs drive business	Customer drives business
Objective customer satisfaction	Objective customer delight/ first call resolution

CULTURE

Before:	*Transformation to:*
Parenting	Partnering
Leadership impeded by administration duties	Management role defined
Focus on performance	Focus on processes and training needs
Unclear selection criteria	Select for core competencies
Mixed messages	Balanced recognition and measurement plans

Benchmarking at GE Medical Systems

GE Medical Systems (GEMS), a medical diagnostic imaging equipment business with world-wide headquarter in Wisconsin and manufacturing facilities in the USA, Europe and Japan, focuses on five broad product lines; ultrasound, X-ray, computer tomography, magnetic resonance imaging, and nuclear medicine. Its services include installation, equipment maintenance contracts, in-house support, part sales and other life-cycle services.

In 1991, the president and CEO asked his management team to start benchmarking other organizations. This request led to a benchmarking study to decide if GEMS should globalize its service parts operations. A team of three came together to identify the 'desired-state' characteristics of a world-wide service parts operation. These characteristics included:

- Unquestioned world-wide leadership in customer satisfaction;
- A global organization with world-class people;

- World-class distribution and networks;
- State-of-the-art replenishment models;
- World-class information systems and;
- World-class asset management performance.

Based on repeated discussion at global part logistics meeting, the team selected 10 areas to benchmark:

- Product life-cycles;
- Network structures;
- Information systems;
- Replenishment;
- Exchange parts;
- Repair facilities;
- Transportation parts identification;
- Performance measurement;
- New product introduction.

Potential best practice partners were selected according to the following criteria:

> They had to operate in global areas, provide a high degree of customer satisfaction *and* have a significant after-sales market.

Based on the selection criteria, nine organizations were chosen as potential best practice partners, all of which agreed to participate in the study. Among the participating organizations were; Caterpillar, Digital, Fuji Xerox, IBM Europe, and Xerox US.

To prepare for the full-day site visits at each of the organizations, the team created a list of questions that were sent to each of the nine organizations in advance. The site visits enabled GEMS to address how to improve overall customer satisfaction. At the end of the site visits, the global benchmarking team summarized the best practices discovered at each company in the 10 different areas. They also identified the gaps between the best practices of the nine organizations and GEMS current practices. Based upon their findings they were able to make recommendations as to how to best close the gaps. From the key findings and recommendations in the 10 areas it became apparent that the way forward would be to create a global operation.

A team was established to address issues surrounding what the global operation would look like. Some of the major outputs of the team included an organizational chart with functional responsibilities together with a manpower plan over the next five years, and an inventory plan with targets for inventory turns, all of which were linked to customer services. A second team was formed to study issues relating to the parts repair operations. At that time the general parts operation had four different repair locations world-wide, which caused duplication of effort and no focus on who might 'own' the repair. Originally the team believed that repairs should be done where the equipment was manufactured. This caused inventory to be moved backwards and forwards throughout the world, since the largest installed base was located in the USA. In view of this the team decided to relocate part repairs to the location of most of its customers. This reduced repair costs, made the customers happier, and allowed GEMS to work as a global organization.

Once the benchmarking team presented its findings of potential benefits together with its plants for implementation, they gained top management support. The next step involved improving the processes. Inventory availability became a big issue. Before the global part operation began, employees in one country had no knowledge that a part existed in the international network. To increase productivity and control inventory, it had to be visible from anywhere in the world at any time.

In October 1992, GEMS developed its global operation with three polar managers representing Europe, Asia and the Americas. All reported to the general parts operation's general manager. Additionally, GEMS created five global process teams under this general manager with culturally-diverse representatives from each global region. The process teams included; service parts supply; customer parts delivery; distribution operations; repair operations and logistics development. In the systems area, GEMS created a world-wide logistics system; global service parts logistics. GEMS's goal was to continue reducing the number of hand-offs and make the process as seamless as possible. The system currently extracts data from the regional systems, reconciles the information and creates a global database that allows forecasting, inventory requirement planning, deployment and visibility on a global basis. This framework ultimately allowed GEMS to trigger an order anywhere in the world at any time and deliver the parts to a field engineer in the shortest time possible.

In pure numbers, the global parts operation reached significant milestones in its quest for world-class status. In four years, GEMS saved $21 million in facility, personnel and inventory reductions. Its number of warehouses decreased by half with the remaining outsourced to warehouse specialists. Inventory turns, defined as the amount of revenue divided by inventory, has increased from 5.1 to 9.6. Before the global initiative, GEMS only had inventory visibility in about half of its warehouses. It now has the capability of 99 per cent inventory visibility. Since the new systems include forecasting modules and tracking systems, it can see inventory from anywhere in the world. Moreover, it is visible to its field engineers who provide the on-site service to its customer's equipment. With the new global focus figures for customer satisfaction also improved. This was experienced across the board in the Americas, Europe and Asia.

This success in pursuit of a global operation involved much hard work by many individuals. Benchmarking initially played a key role to define what other organizations were doing in this capacity. Benchmarking was the catalyst that caused GEMS to recognize that quantum change was possible. By being aware of what was happening outside and adopting or adapting the best practice wherever found, this created a climate for major improvements.

Enquiry handling at the Law Society of England and Wales

The Law Society is the professional body for solicitors in England and Wales and has a dual role of representing and promoting the profession together with regulation of solicitors and their firms in accordance with the Solicitor's Act 1974. The records enquiry service is a section within the regulation and information services department. The section deals with telephone and written enquiries from individual solicitors and their firms, student members, the lending institutions and the general public. The calls range from requests for a referral to a solicitor in a specific geographical or specialist area or checks on whether an individual solicitor has a practising certificate, to queries on the progress of the various applications for certification.

Although there had been earlier disquiet regarding the level of service provided by the enquiry service, it was not until October 1994 that action began to remedy the situation. The new approach was to be more holistic than in the past as it was recognized that the problem could not be solved by simply throwing resources at it.

Position in October 1994

Calls to the service had been steadily climbing from a total of 111,189 in 1991 to 128,379 in 1992. From January to September 1994, 117,749 calls had been received by the service without a corresponding increase in staffing. It was projected, at that stage, that if the trend were to continue into 1995, the department could expect to receive 172,840 calls per annum. Meanwhile, for the period January to September 1994, there were 31,377 unanswered calls. These were callers who had given up waiting in the queue. An increasing number of complaints was recovered from these customers who felt that the society was failing to provide a much-needed service. At times, this put the main switchboard of the Law Society under extreme pressure as it frequently became jammed with callers holding.

The telephony consisted of a PABX system. Calls to the enquiry service were placed into a 'hunt group' in which the call did a circuit of phones within the system seeking someone who would take a call. It was a 'lottery' whether anyone would ever receive an answer. If all lines were busy, the call reverted to the London switchboard operator who asked the caller if they wished to remain holding. The call was then placed back in the queue. This had the unfortunate effect of filling all channels or bands between London and Redditch. To make matters worse, the switchboard over-rode phones which were on 'do not disturb' and where staff were unavailable to take calls for whatever reason. The relationship between the main switchboard and the enquiry service was very poor.

Establishing an enquiry handling service team

This team was established in October 1994, with terms of reference which included looking at radical solutions to the medium- and long-term needs of enquiry handling within the department. It was anticipated that, following the implementation of a new computer system, the Regis system, and building on technology known to be available, options such as voice activated responses or smart answer phones would be considered.

Links with other directorates

In common with the problems faced by the enquiry service, other directorates were facing similar difficulties. In particular, a section with the Legal Practice Directorate was experiencing difficulties with its practice advice line. While the calls were not so numerous, they could be lengthy. Their equivalent to the records enquiry handling team agreed that the existing equipment was far from satisfactory and that plans for an upgrade should be implemented as speedily as possible. The two groups decided to join forces and work towards a solution which would, hopefully, meet their needs.

Exploratory site visits to Glasgow

It was decided that the joint working party could gain a great deal from organizations already successful in this field. Visits were arranged to organizations where dealing with enquiries by telephone was a core business function. A visit to Glasgow was co-ordinated by Ian McPherson of the Glasgow Development Agency who had been instrumental in attracting a high number of blue chip companies to relocate to Glasgow.

As many of these newly established call centres had changed from a face-to-face to a phone-based service, the group was keen to explore what hardware and software had enabled them to do so together with an investigation of the staffing profiles and their policy on training and development. The organizations expressed surprise that the Society used such a high proportion of temporary staff to man front-line help desks. The staff that they employed had been recruited not only on their proven communication skills, but also for their previous commercial experience and educational attainments.

The first organization visit was the newly established BBC Radio Helpline which covers all five BBC Radio networks on a 24-hour, 365 days a year service with staff working in shifts. The service, operating on BT 0800 numbers is free to listeners. The group was impressed by the purpose-built accommodation, the back-up and support for the phone staff together with the powerful computers and large display screens.

The service had invested in the most expert staff it could afford and earmarked a considerable budget for training. Staff were expected to take part in self-study and be fully conversant with changes in their field of expertise.

During the second visit, to the Criminal Injuries Compensation Board, the group discussed with staff the problems with training and meeting the balance between the needs of written- and telephone-based enquiries.

The third visit, to Barclays Shareholding, was quite different from the others in terms of atmosphere. It was almost redolent of scenes within the Stock Exchange. As with the other organizations, there was low turnover of staff and a high quality of those recruited. Although the service was run almost as an assembly line, the needs of the customer were to the forefront and every effort was made to ensure an optimum service. While the BBC service had electronic wall boards advising of the volume of incoming traffic, Barclays used relatively simple, but effective, traffic light systems to alert staff to the number of calls waiting to be answered.

The working party learned valuable lessons from the visits with respect to training, performance and quality initiatives aided internally by staff quality circles. While the working party recognized that the business needs of those organizations differed in many respects from its own, it was also realized that the technology that was being sought had been steadily developing and refining over the previous 10 years. It was no longer cutting edge, but proven by these organizations to have met the needs of large volumes of incoming calls.

Based on the experiences of others, it was recognized that the needs of staff involved in call handling must have a high priority in terms of the equipment available to them, such as large monitors, comfortable rest areas and mechanisms for dealing with what is a stressful and demanding environment. It was felt that the implementation of wall boards would motivate staff because they could see, in 'real-time' what the profile of incoming calls was. Although off-the-shelf software was available for fairly modest operations, customer-built software would provide necessary flexibility to encompass the varying needs of information points throughout the Society. However, a distinct culture change would be needed because the majority of staff who would man a new system, would, at least in the early days, be existing staff who were not employed as call centre staff.

After the site visits

The visits provided fresh impetus for the working party as it was realized that a solution was to be found. The working party felt that the next step would be to develop a comprehensive set of mechanisms for dealing with enquiries of different types and complexities. An essential part of the process would be to investigate the implementation of a good IT solution, direct dial lines, and effective initial targeting of new staff with the right profile.

A detailed profile of customers was built up during a brainstorming session and an attempt made to classify those needs. A 'wish' list was drawn up together with ideas and recommendations for further action.

Immediately prior to the Glasgow visit, the working party had met to evaluate the possibility of an automated call distribution system with a company called Storacall. This would have been a PC-based solution which would have had to be grafted onto the existing PABX system. Storacall was invited to demonstrate the product. The company offered a trial of the system on a group of extensions. It claimed that the system enhanced the working practices of staff and provided a more efficient method of dealing with calls. In addition, managers would have greater control over operations by enabling them to see at a glance where trouble spots in the service were arising. The uniform distribution of calls would eliminate the shortcomings with existing hunt groups.

Outline approval was given by the management board for a pilot spanning the two areas of heaviest incoming traffic, legal education and the records enquiry service. However it was unclear whether this was the correct path to take and people were uneasy that they were on the verge of implementing a costly pilot system without having fully evaluated other options.

Enquiry handling project

A working group was established comprising representatives from several departments: legal education, the records enquiry service, computing and telecommunications, and the internal consultancy unit. Building on the profile of the needs of the two information points, a detailed request for information was prepared and companies were invited to tender for the pilot system. Evaluation of the tenders became a valuable learning exercise as it served to clarify exactly what the business needs were and how these could best be achieved. BT was chosen as the service provider. The main difference between its system and the Storacall system was that it provided the platform for renewal of the entire telephony equipment for the Society. The Meridian system was capable of being upgraded to meet all business needs. In addition, BT had the contract to maintain existing telephony and would, therefore, have a wider understanding of how the pilot system integrated with existing telephony.

A Meridian Option 11 was installed and became operative on 22 July 1996. The system proved to be a great success in terms of managing the flow of incoming calls and generating statistical information to help not only with quantitive performance measurement but also future forecasting of call volumes. Unlike the rival organizations in the bid for tender exercise, the system could be programmed to very fine detail to meet business needs at various seasonal peaks. The ability to provide callers with an interactive voice mail system paid dividends and freed specialist staff from dealing with the more routine and mundane calls.

Introducing the Meridian telephone system

Additional staff were recruited within the records enquiry service for the launch of the new system. Following evaluation of call volumes, legal education also recruited additional staff. The team in the records enquiry service was divided into four areas: dealing with phone calls from the profession and students; the lending institutions; the general public; and a small team which dealt with correspondence but which provided back-up for the phones when needed.

In the weeks prior to implementation, the managers of the two information points underwent extensive training. Much valuable empirical information was gathered from other course attendees with regards to performance measurement, staff rostering, team and individual motivation. A visit to BT's in-bound 152 service, afforded the opportunity to see what the new system would look like.

Developments since implementation

Inevitably, the new system exposed glaring gaps in performance and training within the team. In this, it acted as a valuable catalyst for change. By November 1996, with the appointment of a new departmental manager, it became clear that action needed to be taken to bridge the gap between performance and training. The 21-strong team needed to build a sense of cohesion and focus intensely on the needs of the customer.

A manager and staff working group was established with a brief to look at all aspects of work within the team. In particular, the method of holding and storing information was conducive to fast dissemination of information. Plans for a database of information were set underway. The department hopes to share the information gathered with the rest of the Society to try to improve customer satisfaction across the board.

An improved policy and procedures manual is nearing completion. The work of the service is seasonal with a huge influx of calls in the autumn. Comprehensive plans with regard to the rota on the various teams, comfort and lunch breaks is to be introduced. Four staff were appointed to replace team members who moved, using a new selection and recruitment policy based on recommendations from a training organization, and the best practices of those organizations visited in Glasgow were adopted and implemented. This paid dividends in terms of the process itself and the calibre of the staff appointed.

Conclusions

Whilst the process has been a lengthy one with a few diversions along the way, it has been invaluable in terms of the contacts made, the lessons learned based on the experience of others and the plans which are coming to fruition. BT warned that what may be needed on day one of the new system was unlikely to be the eventual result. In practice, because of the long lead time, the set-up is almost unchanged. Staff working on the section report that their stress levels had fallen as they know that the incoming calls will be distributed fairly by the system. They have an in-built post-call period to give them time to mentally recover before the next call. They have welcomed the discipline involved in working in the call centre and most recognize that they are gaining valuable skills in what is a growth industry. Skills were developed which could be transferable outside the Society. Turnover of staff has been lower than anticipated.

Based on feedback from 'front-line' employees there has been an increase in customer satisfaction. The Society encouraged the use of the direct lines although a large percentage of calls still comes via the switchboard. However, instead of the calls reverting back to the switchboard if unanswered, callers are kept informed by recorded messages and offered alternatives to waiting.

The number of calls taken has increased as the channels between London and Redditch are no longer clogged with calls. Calls taken for 1996 were 175,200 with projections for 1997 to be in the region of 180,000. There remains a worrying number of callers who abandon without getting through. Plans are afoot to spread resources to alleviate this problem. However, most organizations recognize that some callers have a very low tolerance level when faced with a wait on the telephone. Unlike commercial organizations, a 'lost' call does not represent a potential sale which has been lost. The Society prefers to see it as a minus point in terms of customer services. Much remains to be done but the process of incremental improvements continues.

Rosalie Bullock (team leader, record enquiry service)
Gurdip Singh (records and information manager)

TNT UK Limited

TNT was formed in 1946 when Ken Thomas began transport operations with just one truck in Australia. From that time, the company has continued with a rapid programme of expansion throughout the world. TNT started operations in the UK in 1978 when it purchased Inter County Express, a company employing just 500 staff. Since then TNT UK Limited has grown organically to employ more than 9,000 people.

In 1996, the TNT Group merged with KPN NV. The combined operation now forms one of the four largest transport and distribution organizations in the world. TNT UK retains full autonomy in the management and day-to-day operations of its core activities.

There are three major trading divisions, each of which specialises in a particular sector of the transport market. The largest division is TNT Express Delivery Services (known as TNT Express) which offers a unique range of reliable time-sensitive parcel delivery services within the UK. The core business is the provision of on-demand, nation-wide, door-to-door, same-day, and overnight delivery services.

TNT Express employs 5,000 staff and the time-sensitive products carried by the company range from human transplant organs to urgently-required automotive parts.

TNT Logistics provides specialist warehousing and transport for major companies which can justify exclusive use of distribution resources. Customers include blue chip companies such as Rank Xerox, Ford, Shell, Nutricia, DiverseyLever, BT, British Gas, Volkswagen Audi Group, Land Rover and General Electric. TNT Logistics employs more than 2,000 staff and handles a wide variety of goods that are vital to the success of the UK economy.

TNT Newsfast is the leading carrier of national newspapers in the UK. Daily newspapers carried include the *Financial Times*, *Times*, *Daily Telegraph*, *Sun*, *Daily Express*, *Star*, *Guardian*, *USA Today*, *Herald Tribune* and more than half of all the magazines published in that country. TNT Newsfast employs around 1,000 staff and carries 20,000 tonnes of printed matter every week.

Internal and external benchmarking

In 1988, after 10 years of geometric growth, it was time to review, take stock and agree the strategies and policies that would take the company forward to the millennium and beyond. A comprehensive survey of customers and TNT people identified their visions and expectations for the future. A better understanding of company strengths, performance gaps and specific opportunities for improvement was gained. The findings led to some short-term responses such as a simplification of trading structures and the streamlining of processes. More importantly, the survey identified the fundamental issues of customer focus, service enhancement and continuous improvement that have become TNT's core values.

Today, there is internal benchmarking within TNT UK and throughout the TNT Group. External benchmarking extends to competitors and companies identified as being best in class, world-class performers.

Internal benchmarking is based on the key performance indicators identified as the most important factors needed to deliver excellent service to TNT's customers. Weekly measurement and reporting systems have been set up for all these indicators and each location has targets which require improvement from previous best-ever performances. The location indicators are presented in weekly league tables which provide a further opportunity for internal benchmarking.

Sites are rewarded for consistently good performance and for improving upon their previous best scores. By identifying the best-performing and most-improved depots, TNT is able to investigate how good results are achieved so that the best practices can then be passed on and applied throughout the company.

Within the group operations have been benchmarked against other TNT high-performing businesses in Germany, Italy, Canada, Sweden, and Australia. Most of these projects have yielded good ideas for adoption within the business.

Fig 13.1 Benchmarking process model at TNT UK

Select process to benchmark
Process should be critical to succes of the operation
Document existing practice
Identify key performance measures
Select team

Modify process to realize benchmark
Communicate findings to gain acceptance
Develop action plan to close gap
Agree realistic milestones
Report progress to stakeholders
Revise key process measurables
Recalibrate benchmarks

Study who to benchmark
Identify potential partners
Investigate information sources
Determine methods and techniques
Establish basis for information sharing

Evaluate data and determine gap
Compare performance against data
Identify gap type and route causes
Gauge potential future gap levels
Identify difference between current and observed practice
Isolate enablers that deliver superior performance

At least twice a year independent researchers are used to conduct customer surveys of between 3,000 and 4,000 customers. The customer sample groups are selected randomly to ensure statistically valid results and include clients from all locations representing all types of account. The surveys help to identify and improve performances for each of the key customer service features against which results are measured. TNT performance is then benchmarked against the performance of its competitors.

TNT is perceived from these surveys to be superior in 16 of 20 key attributes, and best in every area of the reliability category (which is by far the most important service attribute from the clients' point of view). The main area where TNT is seen to be performing less well is that which concerns price. In the UK transport market there has been a price war and at least six national competitors have gone out of business since 1994. TNT refuses to discount irresponsibly and only competes on the quality of service at sensible prices.

External benchmarking has been performed both against opposition service providers within the industry for specific processes and against some of the top companies in the world for best practices in other areas. Examples of benchmarking include our:

- Delivery service processes with the Swedish post office;
- Employee training activities together with reward and recognition schemes with a major high street retailing organization;
- Health and safety with a leading oil company;
- Credit control with five major competitors;
- Recruitment processes with four organizations drawn from industry, commerce and public sector Industrial Society members;
- Induction training with six other large organizations.

Additional steps have been taken to have the following benchmarked:

- Driver development training by the Institute of Advanced Motorists;
- Sales training by the Institute of Sales and Marketing;
- Supervisory training by the Open University;

- Accident rates against industry figures from the Transport Safety Group;
- Financial results against industry performance from the UK Transport Industry Group;
- Internal training for external exams against national pass rates;
- People survey results against averages from across 450 companies in 18 European countries and against previous European Quality Award winners;
- Subcontract haulage activities with a ready-mixed concrete company;
- Opportunities for improvement suggestion scheme with a previous Baldrige Award winner;
- Environmental activity with a privatized utility.

TNT UK's external benchmarking activity is undertaken by reference to its benchmarking process model (see Figure 13.1). In addition to these benchmarking activities, TNT UK also hosts visits for the Inside UK Enterprises initiative sponsored by the DTI.

TNT was involved in the 1997 European Foundation for Quality Management; and the American Productivity and Quality Centre Benchmarking Consortium study on corporate performance management where it was selected as a best practice company and hosted a site visit.

Current accolades include: the Rover Group supplier of the year award; the Abbey National supplier of the year award; the Unisys/*Management Today* customer care award; and the gaining of an excellent category rating under the Ford Motor Company carrier quality rating scheme.

All TNT UK's QA systems have been certified to ISO 9000 since 1990 and it has won more motor transport awards than any other industry operator. Its quality successes include winning the UK Quality Award in 1994 and the Northern Ireland Quality Award in 1994. TNT UK was also recognized as an Investor In People in 1994 and went on to win European quality prizes in 1995 and 1996.

Tony Curly (director of quality, TNT UK)
Neil Keyworth (information quality manager, TNT UK)

Networking at Virgin Atlantic

Back in 1984, when Virgin Atlantic was established, the operation consisted of a lease purchase on a Boeing 747 and a regular connection from London, Gatwick to New York. Today, some 13 years later Virgin Atlantic has expanded to include on a yearly basis some two million passengers both in the business and leisure markets.

Critical to the success of its operation has been the delivery of a consistent high quality and value for money product. On a continuous basis this is addressed through Virgin's investment in people and aircraft together with its customer focus. Direct customer feedback is obtained from in-flight questionnaires and by holding focus groups. This is balanced by data collated from appropriate external industry surveys. The flight crew is highly experienced and the cabin crew is carefully selected and trained, whilst among its fleet of aircraft Virgin Atlantic has been the first operator to introduce the Airbus A340 and Boeing 747–400 (with General Electric CF6–80 Engines) onto the British Register.

Networking with the Emirates

Virgin Atlantic's success has been actively recognized through various awards including Best Airline of the Year Award (*Executive Travel* magazine) which was won in 1990 and 1991–92 and 1993. In 1994 this award went to the Emirates, an airline that shares many similarities with Virgin Atlantic. Emirates was established a year after Virgin Atlantic in 1985 and on a similar basis; at that time Emirates leased two aircraft from Pakistani Airlines. Today, just as at Virgin Atlantic, Emirates has experienced rapid and successful expansion.

A networking relationship subsequently developed between the two airlines. The relationship is founded on common challenges and problems together with the desire to be the best service on any route that they operate. This has facilitated an interchange of ideas and the free flow of information centred around best practice. Some of the areas where the two airlines have exchanged ideas include:

- Training;
- The use of IT;
- Customer interface;
- Monitoring performance appraisal.

An overview of each of these areas is given below.

Emirates has adopted Virgin Atlantic's approach to training, specifically with regard to the way in which it promotes. Similarly, the way in which Emirates keeps its cabin crew informed through the use of IT provided Virgin Atlantic with the idea on which to base its own cabin crew IT system. The IT system will now become an effective channel of communication through which Virgin Atlantic can ensure that its cabin crew are informed of essential current information, not only in relation to their respective rosters but flight information – for example, in relation to whether a passenger has special dietary requirements. This means that well in advance of boarding a flight, cabin crew is equipped with the relevant information to do its job.

Of significant importance to each airline is the customer interface: in particular the effective monitoring and transference of customer feedback to appropriate individuals. Both airlines have exchanged ideas here, particularly Emirates which operates a team of three departments; the Customer Affairs Department, the Commercial Department and Products Standard Team in the Inflight Service Department; whose purpose it is to audit the quality of product and service on board and at the various stations. This covers everything from technical flaws through to catering, equipment, and service on board. This helps them to achieve a high consistency of product and service as well as react speedily to faults and to passenger criticisms.

Currently, the two airlines are looking at monitoring crew performance. Since the cabin crew is not in an office environment this can prove difficult to assess. Ideas are being crystallized by both Virgin Atlantic and Emirates and these will potentially provide a further opportunity for both airlines to identify and implement best practice.

CONCLUSIONS
The past, the present and the way forward

When we published the first edition of *Benchmarking for Competitive Advantage* back in 1993, in the final chapter we asked the question as to whether benchmarking would go away! Clearly as we argued then, it has not. Benchmarking, after all, is something that we should have been doing, to some extent what we have been doing, for years. Organizations are slow to change, but increasingly there is a recognition that the old functional structures with little cross-functional activity are increasingly out of date, and the question is more about how to implement benchmarking and how to make it a routine part of organizational life.

In broad terms, those who have started will not stop. The surveys revealed that most of the firms expect to do more benchmarking in the years ahead.

It is undoubtedly the increase in commercial awareness that lies at the heart of the benchmarking boom. The competitive pressure to improve the quality of products, service and management effectiveness is clearly a major factor in causing organizations to look for better practice elsewhere. Levels of competition within the US market place and overseas, and perceptions of this competition, have increased greatly in recent years, and, clearly, the same is true in the UK and Europe.

However good benchmarking is, blanket benchmarking is not a sensible proposition. Only small percentages of companies have indicated that they are going to try and benchmark all processes all competitors. The selection of benchmarking partners and processes to benchmark needs to be done very carefully.

Like all new methods appearing on the business scene, benchmarking is not being applied consistently perfectly. Companies clearly have to learn how to do it, when they should do it and what to avoid. Like most new management concepts, there remains evidence of inadequate planning. This is worrying, since unsuccessful benchmarking is frequently the result of poor planning.

Management support is also not always what it should be, despite the fact that surveys tell us that the great majority of the companies engaged in benchmarking had an active total quality management programme. Management education is essential and training is necessary at all levels, particulary for benchmarking teams. Most organizations still consider themselves to be beginners or novices at benchmarking and there is concern as to whether enthusiasm can be maintained.

The sharing of information is a natural part of benchmarking, and does have a major impact on the cost-effectiveness of the approach and the ease of targeting results. Such sharing is helped if information can be kept anonymous or mutual benefit deals are possible. There is a need for infrastructures to be developed to assist this and, clearly, the UK and Europe need an effective equivalent of the American International Benchmarking Clearinghouse. We intend to establish such a European centre at Nottingham Trent University. Quite possibly, small organizations will need special support to help them conduct benchmarking studies given their limited resources and special support is likely to be needed also in the difficult areas for benchmarking, such as the creative service sector.

Finally, as well as a strategy for benchmarking, at the company and at the national level, there is also a need for the benchmarking of strategy. It is not just a question of business processes, physical product and functional areas, it is also a question of how you are going to enter, influence and develop the market; plan, organize and run your manufacturing or service delivery operation; manage a portfolio of interests; structure your development organization; how you are going to survive and grow in the future. We end where we began. Benchmarking is about doing the obvious things in a systematic manner. Consultants cannot 'solve it all'; they can help, but you must own it.

INDEX